Eunoia

NITI MAJETHIA

PARTRIDGE

A Penguin Random House Company

To order additional copies of this book, contact
Partridge India
000 800 10062 62
orders.india@partridgepublishing.com

www.partridgepublishing.com/india

"And tomorrow, it may be, I shall die!...And there will not be left on earth one being who has understood me completely. Some will consider me worse, others, better, than I have been in reality...Some will say: 'he was a good fellow'; others: 'a villain.' And both epithets will be false. After all this, is life worth the trouble? And yet we live – out of curiosity! We expect something new...How absurd, and yet how vexatious!"

- Mikhail Lermontov, *A hero of Our Time*

Eunoia: The shortest English word containing all five main vowel graphemes. It comes from the Greek word εὔνοια, meaning "well mind" or "beautiful thinking."

This book is in memory of one of my beautiful well wishers, my strong and literature-loving grandfather, Ravi Kothari. Voracious reader who liked to write too, once upon a time, a hungry and deeply intellectual mind, one of the strongest and most powerful beings I have ever known and will ever know. I've seen him go through so much...so beautifully, bravely and even more than that, wisely. He is one of my biggest inspirations. He would be one of the most excited people to read my book. I miss you nana, though I know you are within me and I know you are extremely, extremely proud.

Also dedicated to my haters and bullies, for making me feel truly weak and worthless when I was a little child, it is only because of you that I have found my real voice and fought the insecurities to become the totally confident, feisty, passionate and gentle person that I am. Though not an overnight miracle nor a very smooth transformation, (much of what you will come across in the book as you read on) the journey has been beautiful and I have grown closer to writing. Melancholy has drawn me more into the depth of life. Thank you for giving me an opportunity to not just become strong but to also become strength- something my grandfather would be very proud of, actually, is very proud of, today.

Acknowledgements

Immeasurable gratitude to YOU, my dear reader! I may have given birth to this book but it is you that truly brings it to life! Hope this poetry seeps deep into your soul and existence, even deeper than I had to go, in order to excavate these words. Hope this poetry helps you find the treasure chest hidden deep inside you.

As I have mentioned earlier, I am collosally grateful to my grandfather, who is an example of beautiful bravery. His strong mind is what inspires me the most. He went through so much so beautifully...so wisely, so miraculously...and made me believe that I too am as strong as he was.

Thank you, my parents, Shilpa and Hemant Majethia, for putting up with all my insanity, for believing in me so endlessly and loving me even when I'm a total wreck; for letting me freely be myself, express myself, pursue myself...for giving me this life changing, spine tingling and stunning experience of publishing. It may not always be easy being my parents but you both handle it gracefully, which increases my respect for you even further.

It has been an exciting, adventurous and rapturous journey, I have not just grown as a writer but with every book, I know deep inside, I am also growing as a person.

All four of my grandparents, thank you for all the love, pride and acceptance. I am also beyond fortunate to have a strong and supportive family that respects my space, but at the same time is there for me whenever I need them.

Special thanks to my mother (Shilpa Majethia), my nani (Saryu Kothari) and my masi (Kuntal Kothari Thakkar), for giving me your beautiful, old paintings to use in the book! All the doodles, pictures and paintings in the book have been done by these three talented women. Indeed some of the most talented women I've ever met! I feel honoured that your work is able to accompany mine, and that we are emerging as artists in an official publication together!

Joanna Aunty, thank you! Thank you for your tireless effort, your inexhaustible enthusiasm, you are the one who guided me throughout, helped me put this book together and stayed connected to my publishers. You are my manager, agent, editor, friend, teacher and advisor. Thank you for being there those dull evenings when I felt confused and lost a sense of direction, and also those days I was so energetic and happy to work that I wouldn't stop laughing hysterically. Thank you for understanding my style of writing and respecting my work to such a great extent that you actually believed my poetry did not need detailed editing.

All the brilliant people at Partridge Publishing who have worked so hard to turn my dream into reality, thank you, thank you!

My lovely teachers at school who always saw in me something more; who believed I was even capable of what was beyond the curriculum; who encouraged me and stood by me with enthusiasm.

My talented Kidspirit editors in New York, my constantly supportive Indian satellite editorial board members, for believing in me and bringing out the best in me.

My amazing friends, for all the comfort, for being there, always; for putting up with my wild and also Wilde side; for accepting and also enjoying all the strange madness and ecstasy that comes with my friendship.

To ALL the amazingly fantastic people I met in Australia, the fabulous human beings I worked with for the Uplift festival; my supportive audience for accepting me as a public speaker; to the Earth Guardians for letting me participate at various conferences and giving my poetry the wondrous break in an HBO movie! Thank you for believing in me.

To everybody else who has taken the time to know me, understand me, understand my work; to everyone who has believed I could make something more of my life, something beyond- to all those people who were there while I was giving birth to this beautiful little book, to all those people who motivated me and encouraged me to keep going, I value you so much.

To all my inspirations, the celebrities from different fields- Miranda Kerr, Anita Moorjani, Deepika Padukone, Sylvia Plath, John Green, Hilary Duff, Nargis Fakhri, Charles Bukowski, Demi Lovato, Miley Cyrus, Taylor Momsen, Taylor Swift, Lizzie Velásquez, Steve Maraboli, Kirk Nugent, Chip Richards, Luka Lesson, Miss Sadhvi Bhagwati Saraswati- and it's a long, long list! Even all the FICTIONAL characters who have inspired me in certain ways! Which include Veronica from Cocktail, Gordo from Lizzie Mcguire or Serena Van Der Woodsen from Gossip Girl.

To my haters, thank you for hating and hating and helping me actually move forward in my life.

Thanks a million to each little element of nature that has come together and inspired me to go deeper into poetry. I am overflowing with joy because a piece of my heart and soul is going out into the world for the first time...despite the nervousness, there is a beautiful feeling of immense satisfaction and inner peace, because my Art has been calling out to this moment. So thank you, to the Deep Power living in my heart. The only Force I can trust unconditionally. The Outward Force giving me Inward direction. The Inward Force giving me Outward direction. Saraswati Mata, the Goddess of Poetry and Music and whether it is from Shiva, Brahma, Vishnu or Jesus, ALL, Each and Every, equally...the collective power, the invincibly beautiful, unconditional embrace of all the Magic and Gods from every religion and every race, every single aspect of every single universe and every God.

Thank you to EVERYONE living in my heart, from every aspect of the universe to every individual that has added to the person I am today. Every little thing in my life, every small conversation, even the dirtiest and funniest ones, every small touch and spark from and with the universe has helped me discover and develop myself, every little clue has guided me towards the birth and destiny of this book.

And I can assure you, this is only the beginning.

Live dangerously,
Niti Majethia

Foreword

We all touch the edges of poetry in special moments of life…
when the light is just right, when the wind moves through us in
just a certain way, when the touch of a lover or the look of a child
cracks open a doorway inside and transforms our very way of
seeing and being in the world. In truth, poetry is woven through
all of our lives, but it takes a special type of courage to see and
experience life itself in this way. This is the path of the poet, both
dangerous and blessed. If the role of the storyteller is to lead us
on a journey from the mountains to the sea, it is the poet who asks
us to leap from the top of the waterfall and get there in an instant.

I wrote my first poem at 13. It was a simple rhyming piece,
and at the time, was my way of exploring who I was becoming and
who I wanted to be. I can still remember the quiet germination of
the idea, the rush of impulses and the focus of my mind to keep
up with the rhythm of words unfolding on the page. I remember
reading the verses over and over, fascinated. Where did these
words come from? On one hand I felt completely connected to
them, yet their arrival and assembly on the page was somehow
beyond me, a delightful surprise. As a young athlete often
immersed in adrenalin, I was astounded to discover such a rush
of feeling and excitement when all I'd really done was move a
pencil across a page… It felt amazing. I felt alive. Thus began a
journey to discover where else this mystical power of words may
lead. For many years I kept my writing close and shared it with

very few…but eventually came to realize that if this was a journey truly worth taking, it came with a responsibility to share what I discovered along the way.

The book you now hold in your hand comes from an extraordinary young author who has answered the call of the poets path with unrestrained devotion to both harness the creative force within… and to share it with the world.

When I first met Niti Majethia, I was instantly struck by the clarity with which - at such a young age - she has claimed her calling as a poet. Humble but without apology. Selflessly devoted and yet completely self assured. I am a poet. No… I am poetry. Youthful and wise. Subtle and direct. Deeply personal and powerfully universal. Refined and yet alive.

In essence, Niti's work is an expression of the meaning of her title, Eunoia: Beautiful Thinking. This poetry is not an endpoint but a beginning. A doorway. A mirror. It calls for each of us to deepen our own commitment to that which we believe in and to heighten our listening for that which we yearn for. To boldly commit to see the world not only as it is, but as we dream it to be.

I am honored to be the gatekeeper of your journey into this work, and to welcome you to the path of a true poet who shares with us here an invitation to see magic in the world through her lens… and to recognize ourselves within it.

With Peace and Gratitude,
Chip Richards,
Amazon bestselling author of Writing the Story Within

Preface

Firstly, if you're reading this, I'd like to thank you for making it to this page and giving me chance. There is no greater honour for an author than a sincere reader with a hungry and boundless mind.

Eunoia is a word that captured me from the first time I found out that it was the shortest word in the English language to contain all five vowels and it also had a meaning that filled my blood. It is a unique, rare and precious word that even looks beautiful and intriguing in the written form. It literally means "beautiful thinking".

Before we begin, I'd like to tell you a little story. However, after reading it, you can call it a poem if you like, depending on how it impacted you.

There once lived a girl who was strange and mystifying; a mystery within a mystery, a powerful glimpse of tomorrow, a whole world spinning inside her form. Not many people understood her. But those who did, she liked to keep them close. She had so many questions- society said they were unanswerable, but she forgot the most important thing at that point, that she, in herself, was the answer to a lot of her own questions.

Once she discovered that, she began flowing like the wind, becoming a question to a lot of life's aspects, and the world bowed down to her, thus, becoming her answer.

This is how she developed a strange, intimate, secret relationship with the universe, she held the key to unlock a lot of beautiful and tragic secrets. A maiden of honour, she began shining like a star- her teeming light was so powerful that it slowly transformed into a voice. And because she held so much within her, melancholy started to live inside…thus the Gods made her a poetess, her cries became a song, her dreams became a lullaby.

It isn't as complicated as it seems- sometimes you have to watch the sunset alone in order to grasp the power of a goodbye. Sometimes the power of a goodbye will show you the solitude and beautiful colours of a sunset. It is a twisted, fascinating and beautiful life.

In the seventeen years of my life, I have learnt that I don't belong to this world even half as much as I belong to the entire universe, dancing in the whimsical mists of nature. I don't know what's more intriguing, the complexity beyond the horizon or how it all seems to be so simple at the horizon line. Life is a lot like that. We probably don't even know all the complexities underneath the surface, or maybe beyond the surface. But to me, it isn't about living with the moments, it's about living within them.

So I invite you all to live within the skin of the universe instead of on top of it; to truly understand the real meaning of the world according to that little girl in the story; to truly realise what it means to be living, to be drifting, to be uncertain and yet so full of endlessness- the everlasting musical melody of life, its tragic voice, sometimes it doesn't need someone to speak, all it needs is someone to listen.

So deep inside I don't know how these poems came to form, but I guess this is just the universe seeping within me, asking you to stop and look inside, instead of at the outside world we live in. Everybody can live outside but to go within? To go within takes courage, takes humility, takes inward conciousness. And this isn't just a book, this is a journey.

To me, this has been a journey of how I have transformed within some of the most challenging months of my life yet; how I have become the person I am and how it reflects upon this universe; how I create my own magical music when the only instrument I have is my heart. Within this journey there will be answers, questions and lessons that you will probably never even think of.

I think the most beautiful thing about this book is that I never planned it, because it is poetry and as a true poetess, I have let the words guide me, without even once guiding the words. Throughout this book there are random pages and in each of them, there is a question. These are the "Answer this" pages. This is my very own, unique way of connecting with the readers, besides through my poetry.

The little clue I can give you to the answers, is that if you look hard enough and try to analyse the way this book has been created...those pages have been definitely placed randomly, but the template of a MIRROR has been selected by me. This, in itself, is a very big clue.

Why?

Because the answer is within you!All you have to do is reflect.

To me, this poetry is beyond expression, beyond impression, beyond anything you can imagine- mainly because it comes from a part of me that nothing else can reach besides poetry, music and words.

Deep from the bottom of my heart, whoever you are, wherever you are, whatever you are, I hope you can reach out to the depths of your existence and just feel the music coming out... the music beneath the skin and muscle of life, beneath the flesh and bone- the whirlpool of magic, the tireless heartbeat of intuition, of adventure, of emotion, of purpose.

You, my reader, are beyond what can ever be read. You, my reader, are beyond what can ever be said. The unspeakable tales of the history of your very own existence, the baked beauty of this universe in the oven of God- everything has to go through heat, and so do you.

So what do you do?

Turn your sweat into art.

This is more than my sweat and blood, this book is the very meaning of the seventeen years of my existence.

A meaning you'll never find in the dictionary, even though it contains just words, although this book contains just words, too.

I hope after reading the book, you understand the difference between both.

~ I'll be seeing you,

Niti Majethia

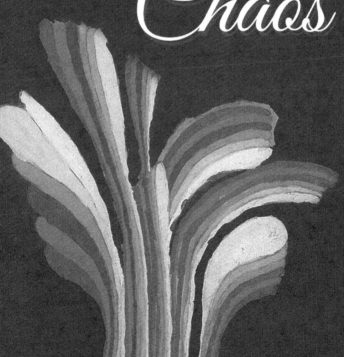

Magical Chaos

I think we go through so many different experiences, different emotions and different aspects of life but mostly it's all through the same dimension of perspective. It isn't about what we see, but how we see it. It isn't about how we are, but how we can be what we dream to be. Life holds so many puzzles and beautiful substances that it translates into something so meaningful if only you put in your heart and soul into really understanding yourself. But most of the time, you just have to live- and hope that life will fill for you different essences to touch, so you feel the very same life, but with different textures. For is there any bigger prison than our very own life? Imagine living beyond our life, beyond this set up- not just beyond society, but beyond everything that has happened and everything that is yet to come. It seems like no matter what we do, we can never escape the person that we are.

So what do we do?

We keep growing, we keep evolving, we keep enhancing- hoping someday, all of this will make sense. But it isn't up to us for it to always make sense. Sometimes the dictionary is in itself the meaning, because when the road is bountiful and meaningful, a destination is irrelevant. And that is life. All you have to do is let the roads guide you, but at the same time know when to guide the roads. You have to let the worlds of emotion come together and touch upon your soul and also touch you beyond your soul. You have to let things happen, you can't always be the one happening. Sometimes you have to go with the flow; sometimes you have to take control and become the flow. Everything depends upon how your life shapes up. How you shape up, what you are and what you are here to become, what you choose to become.

There is so much underneath the crust of this journey we are on. Deep down, deep inside the core, there is a stirring silence-calling out not our name, but the very truth of our existence. Why were we put here? I'm not looking for a meaning. I'm not looking for an answer. I'm looking for a real question. Is God giving us a clue? Who are we?

There is so much within us that is inexplicable. There is so much detail on the sculpture and within each detail is a different hint as to who we are here to be and what we are here to become. The secret of life is this: everything depends on the world you create. Every form of painful friction can light a spark; every heartbeat is a silent spirit coming from the magical chaos of this universe. So what do you do? Listen. Listen. Listen. It's a calling.

It's an inevitable song that knows how to sing only through the tune of your name. You are your own melody, don't be afraid to be. You were here to be a plot twist in the world's novel, don't be afraid to be. This is the magical chaos. Don't be afraid to be, and you will be remembered not just for all you were but for how you became that, how you kindled your own spark and lit a candle even when you were scared of fire.

Are we Ants?

How miraculous
and overwhelming it is,
that for the little
ants on the ground
even the tips
of leaves
sparking off moonlight
on the branches
can become stars.

Crumbling

The waves
that crash the hard rocks
ruthlessly and stubbornly
are indeed a blessing
because they contain
the wetness to soften
the rock.

Worlds apart

He is what reminds people
of the serenity of the lakes-
and I am the reason lonely people
find a strange comfort
in the volume
and the destruction
of the high tide.
I am the monster of the sea,
I have a voice.
I am the reason people
find communication,
he is the reason people
find stillness.
Even though we were
both inexplicably different,
we were both loveable,
for there is so much to learn
from the determination of the storm
and so much to seek
from the reflection of the lake.
Just like all people,
holding their own
endless possibilities
and tides-
there is a different experience

in the journey of each person.
Don't undermine difference,
this is the experience
that will eventually
give you clues,
to the landscape
of your very own destination.

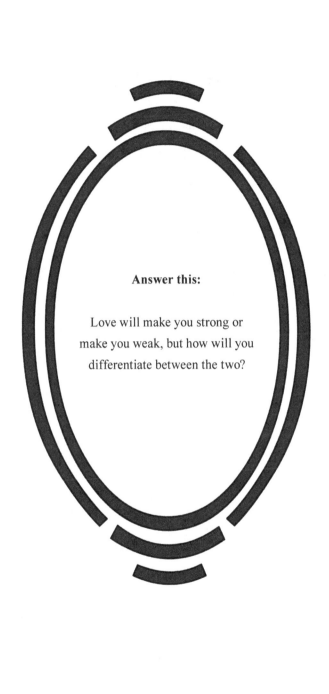

Answer this:

Love will make you strong or
make you weak, but how will you
differentiate between the two?

Dry and Wet

Maybe the waves
are dancing
to the music
the tide is playing-
a sweet song
of melancholy and escape
that we cannot hear,
but we can feel it,
the first time
the waves roll in
and kiss our dry feet,
the first time
we understand
the real meaning
of being touched.

Endless

It's like God is watching over us,

but we are still so free!

What a wide, vast, lone universe!

Opening up new horizons

and widening the ocean

of possibilities!

Oozing with synchrony,

yet drifting in

the arms of melancholy!

All these emotions,

bitter and sweet-

all this love,

all this hate!

All these oceans

rising and falling,

this is what it is to be alive-

this is what it is to

have a beating heart,

just like a drifting tide,

up and down,

and I am in myself an ocean-

meeting so many rivers

and making love to the horizon!

And yet, there are so many hidden things

we can find inside our own stillness!

Inside our own sweet quiet space-
there are so many silences
that have their own song!
The wind, the sky, the sea-
where are we?
Where are we going to go?
Are we going anywhere, at all?
What is the distance to death?
Is it really just measured
by the number of years?
Is it really just measured by time?
Are we Time?
Does Time run because of our existence?
Does our existence run because of Time?
Who are we?
What is Time?

Flowers

When the flower

opens up,

it looks as if

it is yawning-

waking up

from a dream

so fulfilling

and enriching

that only its

fragrance remembers.

And thus it sings, sings

bleeds its poetry out-

this is the art of the dreamer,

to express,

to intoxicate,

beyond our thorns,

beyond our small body.

Windows of life

The dense forest
may be dark,
but then again,
it allows you to appreciate tiny
gaps of pouring light,
from all the different places,
from tiny gaps
in the oozing trees
and nothing ever feels empty,
nothing ever has a gap,
for gaps are windows-
to welcome more,
beyond the fright.
Once you learn to see it right,
once you learn to see beyond sight,
once you follow the moon
straight into the night.

History

History
reminds us
of evolution
but it is only
if we look
in ourselves
can we realise
the meaning of
true revolution.

Looking into Love

Maybe Love
isn't about finding
an answer-
it's about
becoming a question.
Maybe Love
isn't about the cold
never being there,
it's about
never feeling it.
Maybe the World
doesn't write your story,
but you write
your story upon the world.
It is with your essence
that the world comes up,
that the world becomes,
the world glows
with the light
of your shine.

Oceans of thought

The ocean
has waves and ripples
just to show us that
even though
the path of life
may not be smooth
and straight,
it can still be beautiful.

Poetry

Poetry-
always the perfect
combination
of fantasy and reality,
a story
built on
the foundation
not of only unspeakable answers,
but also unanswerable questions.

Softening Winds

Every whisper
of the wind is a story-
but the tingling
feeling it gives you?
the way it touches you
and brings to you
the real resonating reason
for being alive?
That is a real poem.

Being Me

Under my skin

there is literature

which can be read

from the reflections

of the light in my soul.

In my heartbeat

there is a tide

which will meet the horizon

when my passion

becomes the sky of my life.

I run wild and

it isn't easy

living in my head.

But oh my unconditional God,

who would be able

to handle it,

if not me?

I am the ultimate ocean

that is fearless

and boundless.

I don't want to just touch the sky

I want to kiss it to the point

that it starts to swell

and it starts to rain

so that I can watch all

the raw and beautiful
plants around me
spring to life-
so that I can sing along
with their fragrance
and make my own
song that plays along with
the music of the wind.
I want to let the wind
break through all my scars
and accept my every atom
as it is.
I want hunger. I want rapture.
I want confidence. I want laughter.
More than everything, I want more passion.
What more can one want?
I want to hold the stars
so gently that their light
fills up the craters of the moon.
I want to feel everything-
from the beginning of happiness
through the life of good old Time,
towards the end, which is dying stars
and bursting black holes-
or fire or ice.
I want to hold all these words
inside me
and let them burst

like a rainbow
I just want to live my life
like the horizon
has the meaning
of my existence
written upon it.

Stars Run Wilde

Stars

run wild

in the old

heart of the sky

like emotions rushing by.

They may be painful

and may hold old

past lives,

but at the end of the day

they are all so fragrant

with the kiss of light,

humming the soft lullaby

of the night.

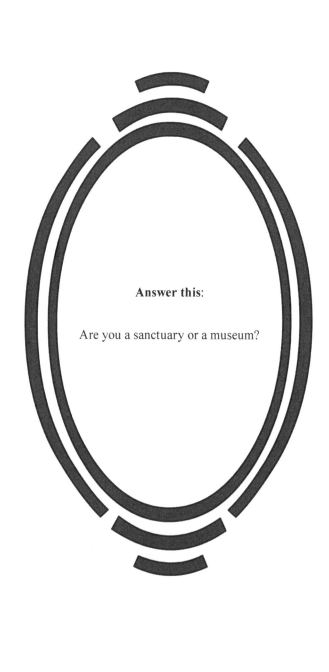

Answer this:

Are you a sanctuary or a museum?

The Biography of the Ocean

The ocean doesn't stop
to see what the shore thinks about it.
It keeps drifting on
in its own musical melody,
dancing within the spirit
of its own wetness,
rises after it falls,
its up and down motion
instantly pushes it forward,
toward something more,
toward the horizon.
And that is why
the sky doesn't mind
reflecting its own
colours upon it.
And that is why
even when it is still,
trying to kiss the horizon
in the literal sense,
in reality we know
it has already made love to it,
simply because it etches out
beyond distance
and lets its passion flow forward.

The Fibre of Melancholy

Because darkness
makes discovery so
much more interesting,
because a world
isn't born
without collision,
without a loud bang,
because dropping
down on the floor
allows you to
plant your own seeds,
because tears
can grow new plants, too.
Scars are the lines
that can start a new artwork,
a new network!
Because rails of blood
turn into lines of a poem.
Because light makes things burn
but it can also make them shine.
And you can be your
only shine and hopefully,
the heat will warm
somebody's soul.

The History of Existence

The sea isn't perfect,
it holds ripples and lines,
and yet it can draw a feeling
of overwhelming love and wetness
at the shore-
where the two states of matter meet,
where forms of love touch.
It may not be perfect,
yet it can communicate with the sky
and send its love,
yet it can reflect the beauty
of God's colours upon its surface,
reflecting the sky,
and if you dig deeper,
it reflects the beauty
of God's soul,
with the pearl
specially sealed in the oyster.
The sea may not be perfect
but it still holds itself gracefully,
kissing the river
and bonding with the horizon endlessly-
pushing itself forward
in the deep realms of universal discovery,
it may not be perfect
but it is always alive
with the spirit of its tide,

it may not be perfect
but it holds an impeccable notion of life,
it holds more life
than any other form of matter ever seen-
it endures its relationship with the sky
and as easily as it gives love,
it also takes love-
in the form of rain,
it lets the bullets of raindrops
hurt because love hurts,
it lets them flourish
and fill it up with even more,
because isn't that what love is about?
It reflects life upon the horizon
and it returns to the shore
like it has a promise to keep,
like it needs the touch of the shore's reality
to help it surge even deeper
within its own dream,
it flows in desperation sometimes,
like it needs a voice to translate
all that it is feeling,
like it needs answers
to the question that it is-
an unspeakable anecdote of mystery,
Where did it come from?
How does it endure?
This is your life.
This is the whole of humanity.

The Human Mysteries

Our souls are all connected-
and yet, we experience
each emotion so differently.
What an adventure!
We let our whole souls develop
upon what we feel-
what we absorb.
Our senses are avenues
that the world explores-
or vice versa.
Either way,
what about the colours beyond
those our eyes are capable enough to see?
What about the emotions beyond
those which our soul is capable enough to feel?
What about the mystery inside,
the depth and truth that lives on
which we are not yet able to reach?
God has made us with so many little secrets-
we hold so much within.
Have we made use of all of it?
Have we used even a little, at all?
What is your definition of little?
What is your definition of this world?

The Loves of Life

When the sun and moon are aligned-
the forces of attraction are very high,
thus the tides are dramatically high and low,
much like Love within our life.
It isn't about controlling the tides,
it's about celebrating the fact
that each tide brings
its own type of motion,
its own type of movement,
and each type of movement
brings its own kind of inner revolution.

The Paths of Light

Lightning is never
a straight line
because it shows
that even a path
that does not go
straight ahead,
has the ability
to shine
and illuminate the sky.

The Secret of the Crescent Moon

The crescent moon
is a line of a poem,
so strong,
holding so much meaning,
so much power,
that even though the darkness
has twisted it
and changed its shape,
this connection of its words
still has the powerful
dedication and essence
to shine on.

The Wind's Whimsical Being

The wind
touches everything-
in its skin
it carries stories,
histories from
all that it senses,
these anecdotes
transform into
the magical embrace
used to cool someone,
those morals
turn into
songs that it sings
in order to make
the trees dance,
in order to carry
pollen that gives birth
to even more stories,
with a new essence,
a new theme.

What Living Feels Like

The soil
that everybody
steps on
is the same soil
that allows seeds
to sprout,
to germinate,
to grow.
Imagine the strength
of this earth,
cultivating growth,
holding so many souls,
absorbing so much life-
carrying the weight
of haunting death
and keeping them
all in one place together,
holding a sincere madness
in all balanced sanity,
holding a new horizon
in all old charm.
Holding pride and gratitude
with pure grace,
holding answers with no
questions amongst all solace.

This earth, how magnanimous it is!
How wide and vast and boundless!
How it holds invisible
and invincible winds,
highlighting the importance of
feeling, not looking.
How it holds unspeakable answers
and unquestionable treasures!
Have we even peeked in?
Have we ever tried?
Have we gone that one step further
and learned to truly live our life?

Mysteries of the Waterfall

The waterfall
falls so fearlessly
knowing that it may join a river
and even if it doesn't,
it will walk alone
and become its own
flowing river.

Autumn

Autumn is losing everything-
yet there is so much
red flaming beauty in that loss.
Autumn is to welcome
the arrival of spring.
Autumn is to let go of things
as they dry and fall to the ground.
Autumn is to be bare,
naked, vulnerable.
Autumn is to realise that
it is only in solitude
that the real skin of your bare branches
can feel the moonlight.

Depth within Darkness

What depth has ever existed
without darkness?
The deepest woods are dark,
the deepest of the oceans are dark.
the deepest of nights hold the darkest of fibres
that tether their way to find light.
What depth has ever existed
without darkness?
It isn't about fighting the darkness,
it's about finding a meaning within it,
a meaning so true that it forms light,
just like the night.
You don't even have to try
or stress over it-
your life will recognise the light easily,
especially because life is made up of it.

Within
and Without

Within and Without

I don't know - I think of what I want to do in the future and I believe that I don't just want to be a typical poet. I want to be a poet, but within that, I also want to be a poem. I want to be a public figure, in order to inspire and reach out to a wider audience. But at the same time, I want to keep my secrets close and tuck them softly within my words. Let the readers find clues and let those clues lead them to their own secrets within their own life. I want to speak and talk and dress with my style. I want young girls out there to know that it's okay to be you. I want to be an example of that. I want to be an example of how even if you ever have flaws, you can be beautiful. You can be poised. You just have to be you. I have so much in me that I need to let out. Step by step. Meet people, do things. I want to be so much more than what they think I will be. Or even what they expect me to be. I think I'm lucky to be where I am and more than that I'm lucky to be where I dream to be, in my imagination. It takes less than a minute for me to escape and I think that's one of the things I'm most thankful for. I think it doesn't matter how far you can swim, but what matters is how deep you can push against the currents and reach out to the inner ground that people don't notice, that people usually step on. I think it's all about what's within. Without the within, there is no winning. I want to be myself, fierce, confident and feisty, but at

59

the same time reserved to a certain extent, gentle, compassionate and endlessly kindhearted. I want to look within and find clues that lead me to my destiny. And I want that for all of you. When I see my readers, I don't see people- I see their destinies. I can't say who you're going to marry but I can surely say you are worth loving, and you will find that love someday. Just look within, an endless gleam of hope and possibilities spring up when you look at your soul dancing to the rhythmic enchantment of the universe. You are here because you are meant to be. Now look outside! It's all wild and free. Immerse in the lovely tune of being alive, look within, look outside- everything is in sync, everything is coherent- let it all flow, inside there are answers you still don't know...

A Special Message for the Reader

The stars are stories
the sky is telling-
with the light being
the moral.
The fragrance of a rose
is its poem,
with the thorns
being the meaning.
The constellation is a song
and the dying stars are the tune-
if the night is the world
then YOU are the moon.

Treasures of Life

Treasure

is hidden deep

inside the earth

because the truest

and rawest form

of belonging

is hiding

within our own depths.

Darkness

There is something
so mysterious about darkness-
an unrevealed thought,
a secretive answer
or question.
The light reflects upon everything
and makes it shine,
but the darkness of life?
There is so much
to search for within it.
Darkness encourages
us to turn on
our own inner light
and try to look carefully
at the little things.
The light shows it,
but it is the darkness
that teaches us
to find our own way.
So much moonlight
comes down as poetry,
but still leaves us to wonder
and be consumed
within the quest
of darkness.

The moonlight of life
directly reveals only
what it wants to,
these are little clues-
but the rest we have to
discover by ourselves.
And at the same time,
we also discover ourselves.

Depth

The deeper in the soil you go
the richer the nutrients you find.
Have you gone deep inside?
Now think about the hardness-
the hardest and toughest
of substances can,
too, be beautiful.
Diamonds,
the hard rocks
deep inside the earth
that look like crystals and artworks
of nature's finger tips.
The deeper into your existence you go,
you will find darkness
amongst your roots.
But there will be nutrition,
there will be growth,
there will be old rocks
that are hard and difficult
but within them
is just so much beauty,
substance and matter,
within them
there is a whole breath of God.

Earthly Values

The earth
is our connection
with God.
It was created for us,
we were created for It.
Only if we could understand
that the earth is honesty
in its purest form,
the flowers don't hide their rot,
the wind doesn't hide its song,
the sky never hides its thunder.
The world is a vast and free
source of energy,
of scars and wounds,
of beauty and acceptance.
The bird does not wonder
how others feel
about its song,
about its voice,
it just sings to drown out the noise.
It sings honestly.
It sings with its heart.
And when it sings,
even the wind dances along,
transmitting the sound that we hear,

bringing to us
a song of nature,
the birds,
the pure truth of being.

Answer this:

There is a universe in your mind beyond
what you think, there is a whole galaxy
within your soul beyond what you feel.
How will you explore the rest of the world's
secrets within your unconsciousness?

Echoes

An echo
is the most beautiful
form of an ephemeral memory-
even though it isn't
the real first time voice,
it's still holding
so much of that moment,
like a distant form of truth,
like a momentary memoir.
I hope my voice
is strong enough
to become an echo
that reaches the stars,
so that they learn
to shine with the light
of my words.
But most of all-
I hope my work
carries the echo
not of my speech,
but my heartbeat,
not of just the will of my destiny,
but also the immense power
of my dreams.

Flaws

Little, tiny drops of rain
may look like pimples
on the flower's skin
but it's so ironic-
it is those drops
that cool the flower.
Flaws are the rawest
and most original forms of you,
how "cool" is that!

Let the Wind run

The sky stretches out
as vast as your own imagination,
and maybe the sky
is somebody else's ground,
maybe the clouds
are somebody else's soil.
Plant your seeds everywhere-
because you may not even know it,
but pain
often comes in the form of rain,
when the cloud
has had too much to bear.
Don't forget that thunder can
be its own kind of music
and lightning can
be its own form of colour and paint.
Remember that darkness
is its own kind of story
and the moral lays
only within your own,
naked and vulnerable soul.

How well do you Know Life?

Maybe mysteries
aren't about connecting the dots,
but making something of them.
That is beyond just dots,
that is beyond just mystery.
Such is life.
You go through each day-
but what becomes of each day?
Where do you go
if you want to get out of your life,
out of your body?
What do you call home,
when your heart is lost,
when your mind has forgotten
what the soul remembers,
when your soul cannot relate to your mind?
Maybe we are all the stars
and God is the starlight.
Whatever we illuminate,
is through His light-
but at the same time,
we hold our own type of shine,
an authentic, individual,
invitation of life.
It is all so immense,

we are all made

by the same Creator,

yet we are all born

from different dimensions

of perception,

of thought,

of essence!

We are all made

in the heart of Him-

in the richness of truth

and purity of living.

This is your raw form.

This is your ethereal, eccentric

and most real form.

Everything else is just a mask.

Don't role play.

To be most beautiful,

let your heart

be in your most natural state.

Wear your confidence in your eyes.

Let your soul see what you can't.

Let your mind discover what isn't really there-

make up what you want.

Live inside it.

Looked inside?

Put your foot
on the ground lightly,
with love,
each step with poise.
There could be seeds under
your sole,
under your soul.

Meanings beyond the Dictionary

What is the real meaning of life?
What is the real meaning of existence?
Of the good, the bad,
the mortal beauty on this planet?
If it were all to turn to dust-
why is it created?
Are we to leave back
something that can never fade away?
What can never fade away?
Art?
Science?
Legend?
If everybody
has a different meaning of life,
how are we all still living together?
Maybe that is the real beauty-
to be able to see life
through different windows
and maybe life doesn't change,
but the tint on the window does.
Maybe the world is a whirlpool of questions
and we are answers.
Each of us,
seeking deep into the darkness
of our existence,

looking inside-

looking for answers

to be translated,

and what is the language of existence?

Is it love?

If love is the language of existence,

why is there so much

hate in the world?

What are the truths

hidden in the darkness?

But even more than that-

there must be the deepest

secret hidden in the light,

in our everyday lives-

a clue we overlook,

something we ignore,

is it the beating of our own hearts?

Whatever it may be,

it brings us one step closer

to the real, fundamental definition

and reason of existence,

not just for the human race-

but for all living species.

Ocean's Literature

The ocean's literature
is thrust upon its surface,
drawing in and bleeding out
with the tide.
However only if you swim
deeper inside,
within the darkness,
you will find life,
you will find growth,
within that darkness,
you will find
the real meaning
of this literature,
the honest truth
of being alive.

Star Gazer

The stars are poets
with the light
being the poem-
the light illuminating
and uncovering
so many secrets
of the deep night,
the light being
a guiding force
to enchant
the long lost travellers-
the light
being a sign
that even when all seems dead,
something is alive.

The Fruit of Living

But be brave
enough to peel
off the skin,
and inside
lies a whole
gorging, juicy universe
of nutritious passion.

Answer this:

What we know is only through our
senses; what about the things that
the human system cannot translate?
What about those little secrets that
may be a code to our destiny?

The River Maiden

The beautiful body of the river
gracefully moves on
into every phase of life,
every form of landscape,
even though there are rocks,
even though there are trees.
All you really need is the current.

The Truth about Beauty

Maybe beauty isn't
about looking at,
it's about looking beyond.
Maybe beauty isn't
about the stardust,
it's about the dust
that can look like stars,
just by daring to fly
and letting the light shine through.
Maybe beauty isn't
about the people who have it all-
it's about the people
who have nothing but imperfections,
but wear their imperfections
so gracefully
that they don't need fashion statements,
as they become style statements.

You are a Strawberry

The strawberry
may have holes on its skin,
But when you crack it open
and look into the heart of it,
there is the white
that has an immense softness,
that has the beauty
of mixing with the red
so effortlessly,
and that white
makes the strawberry
feel like it is glowing,
effortlessly and flawlessly,
bringing out its nutrients.
At the surface of the strawberry
it may have its holes-
but deep inside,
it holds a story untold.

How to love someone deep

Maybe the ocean is deep
Because its lonely limbs are looking
for someone brave enough
to push against the currents
and feel the deepest of depths
while experiencing that love-
that intense passion,
that breathless grace.
Maybe the ocean is deep
because for once
it wants to make someone feel
like it is meant to be explored,
not just opened.
For once it wants to feel
someone diving inside it,
with the hope of finding
a different state of matter in their own soul,
with the hope of finding flow,
with the hope to find rhythm in the current.
And that is the meaning of being deep-
so that the person that is brave enough
to fall inside you
doesn't just find,
but discovers.

All

things

connected

All Things Connected

At some points in your life you will feel uprooted from your environment. You will feel like a total misfit; defeated, broken, weak and absolutely misunderstood. This is the disconnection that is a voice calling out for you to listen to the real, inner connection.

I've had times in my life where I've had so much anxiety- it gets hard to even breathe. I've felt unloved, even worse, unlovable! And misunderstood, and a lot of times, I've felt absolutely nothing. The intensity of emotion is great. You may never have to face the kind of internal struggle I do.

But we all need to realise that the point when we feel disconnected from the world, is that point when we move a step closer to the universe.

I feel misunderstood all the time, even with most people who are closest to me. But at the end of the day, that's what made me connect to nature, to the universe, my thoughts mirror those reflections, my inner world was a part of a different dimension that I discovered through poetry. Because at the end of the day, is this not what we are? We're all made up of the same components- the universe gracefully demonstrates that.

And who are we to challenge this Truth? Lord Shiva (or any God that you believe in, or all the Gods!) have made us all parts of the same nature, this brings us all so close, no matter what the differences are.

One experience I've had in the seventeen years of my life that made me feel connected to ALL things in the universe was at the Uplift festival at Byron Bay, Australia. Since I work with the Earth Guardians and spread awareness about protecting the environment through my poetry, I was one of the chosen five youth leaders from around the world to come and launch the 'global alliance of youth in action' portal. Flattered, of course, I had no idea what to expect. But that experience really changed me; the way I interacted with my readers, my co-workers, the way I see the world. Everything seemed to fall into place and I was truly uplifted as a human being in terms of goodness and spirituality. That is when I truly learnt to love myself and take care of myself. So many different people of different cultures and so much beauty, so much wealth of the heart, so much richness in being. I met so many people that have forever changed me and helped me become a better person, not just toward myself but also toward the world and the universe.

It is important for all of us to realise we are all made of matter, of atoms, we are living beings. We are more than things, we are called beings because we must "be". Join me in the journey of being, of transforming, of becoming- but more than that, of realising, of discovering within us and revealing the connected universe around us.

A Memoir of the Heart

Maybe the birds
are the sky's thoughts
going deeper
in its whirlpool of colour
and uncovering its secrets.
For our thoughts reveal to us
spaces of our soul
we never knew existed-
our precious thoughts
bring to us
pieces of an existence
we didn't fully know.
A thought is more
than just a product
of the brain.
It's also a memoir
of all that the universe
has buried deep inside you,
parts of you
that you can't see
but they ooze out anyway-
as secrets
waiting to be revealed,
to be stripped off,
naked-

until all we have inside
is silence,
pure, raw silence,
which, inevitably,
is the biggest secret
in all of the universe.

Accepting Life

The sun
controls all the colours
and the sky wears them
all so gracefully.
The sky oozes out
all its inner colours
and the sun
accepts and shines
through them
so effortlessly.

Absolute honesty

I don't have anything negative
towards anybody at all,
especially not God.
Any God. All Gods.
I get a lot of bad thoughts,
but at the end of the day
I just want to thank God for all I have
and for all I am yet to acquire.
I want to thank Him for all I am
and all I am yet to become.
I don't want to be morbid.
I don't want to be rude and shallow.
I want to be kind
but confident and tough,
I want to flow freely
into this universe-
like the wind,
I want to create storms
only to showcase my lightening
and I want the thunder
to turn into music.
I want to add to the beauty
of this world,
and enrich all the heavenly paradise
that already exists.

I want to see more,

be more,

and become more.

I want to know

the parts of myself

within this world-

the outer world

guiding me into

my own inward movement.

I want to unravel the earth

and put it back together again,

uncover mystics

and cover them

while they reveal

my own inner essence.

I want to drown

in misery

and be surged within happiness,

only to experience all

sides, tones and shades of life.

I want to know more,

feel more,

see more-

I want to grow.

Grow beyond and outside

the horizon.

Shed my pain

and fly with the wind.

I wish I could explain this
even better.
I wish I had words
for all the times
I have cried myself to sleep,
for all the times
the anxiety has crept up
and tried to choke me,
for all the times
I have glided in happiness,
for all the times I have died
in pain
and actually felt reborn.
I wish I could explain
more than words can,
I wish I could live my life so honestly
that even nature
begins to feel like
it has somebody
who's growth corresponds.
But no matter what happens,
I know He lives within me.
I know He does.
He breathes
and flows within me.
Within me,
He thrives.

Constellations

They say the constellation
of stars holds meaning,
that they come together
to tell a story-
that the night
of the aligned stars
is the luckiest.
This is just the sky
trying to tell us
to come together
despite our culture,
our background,
our religion-
to form a constellation
of Humanity,
of living,
a constellation
of souls and nature,
of the trees, of the stillness
and peace,
so that the earth, too,
forms a meaning,
so that the earth, too,
tells a story,

so that the earth, too,
is a lucky form of alignment
in the sky
of all the universe.

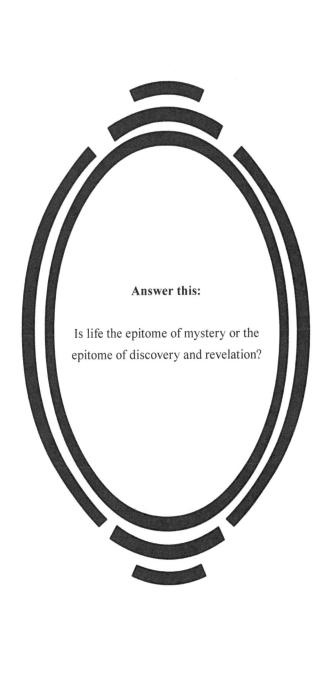

Answer this:

Is life the epitome of mystery or the
epitome of discovery and revelation?

Different Types of Trees

The trees are all green
but all different types of green,
with different adaptations,
designs and creativity-
yet, each of them
have their own beauty
and shade.
Each of them
have a way of making
the nutrients in the soil
feel valued, feel worthy.
Each of them
can reach deep, deep
right into the core
of the earth,
listen to life's beating heart,
listen to the earth's soul
and it is because they can
seep so deep into the soil,
within their silence,
deep into the core
of all our lives,
deep into the earth-
because they have the ability
to feel and absorb,

can they gain the energy

to fight the heat

and transform

the light,

can they gain

the energy

to create the fruit

that will once again,

leave back its own seeds,

its own enduring

promise of growth.

Free

You are one with nature-
your heart beat is the tide
and the rhythm of the pulse
is your current,
your breathing
is the drifting dreams
discovering an endless horizon,
and your ocean
kissing the river
is an ignition of love,
two extremely different
water bodies
coming together as one,
and that is our world,
that is our destiny.
The wholeness of the ocean
even after evaporation,
that is who you are.
You,
yes you,
a member of the human race-
nature's endless form of grace.
The ocean plays its music
with its up and down motion,
like piano keys

melting upon the endlessness

of this world-

and sometimes,

you must remember-

that it is the heat

that will make you evaporate.

It is bearing the burning

that will set you free.

Freshly baked stories of the forest

The forest
weaves its own
little tent around,
with all the leaves and branches
of different trees
knitting inside each other
and making love.
But there is always little light
that peeps in
through the tiny, empty spaces
between the trees
and tickles
the dark, dusty and deep world
of the forest
in order to illuminate
its beauty.
There is always
the universe doing
its little things
in order to enchant
the best of you
and the best in you.

Innermost discoveries

The ocean is like paint
on our globe-
look how much life
it holds within,
the constant movement
of exploration,
the urge to discover
and find something more
on the shore
than just sand.
There's so much within
all this dancing-
all this whimsical
music calling
and chanting.
Maybe our world
is not a piece of Art,
but a form of Art-
a medium of expression,
that cultivates its own artists-
and we are all a part of that,
just by living
in this world.

Little Things

Only the darkness allows us
to truly admire the light.
Only going deep in the ocean allows us
to truly explore the hidden life inside.
Only the light teaches us
how to be everywhere-
yet never completely reachable.
Only the wind teaches us
to whisper even the softest notes
and not make them listen, but feel.
Only the red roses show us
the beauty of thorns
and the thorns show us
the beauty of becoming strong.
Only the dawn shows us
the beauty of a beginning
Only a dusk shows us
the solace of an ending
For only a dusk
can introduce us to the stars.
Only the moon shows us
the meaning of being quiet
yet saying so much.

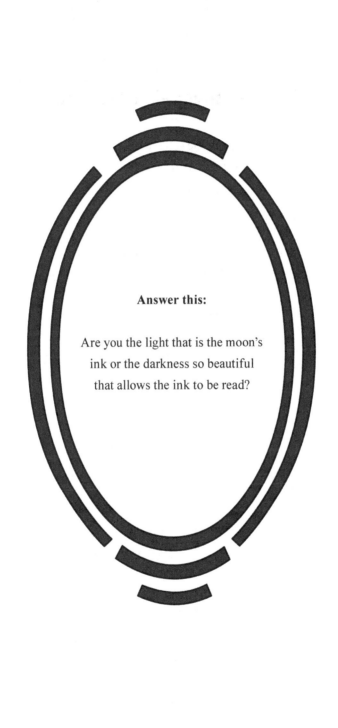

Answer this:

Are you the light that is the moon's
ink or the darkness so beautiful
that allows the ink to be read?

Lord Ganesha's Breathing

Maybe the soft wind
that disperses seeds
comes from
Lord Ganesha exhaling
his love upon the world
and giving out only purity
for the birth of a new crop,
so that there is growth
garnered on this earth
in the form of
juicy and edible substance.

Meet the wind

The wind

is another form of God,

everywhere,

touching everything,

carrying pollen

so gracefully

in order to

let there be more bloom,

so secretly,

tickling your hair

in order to make

you feel more beautiful,

everywhere,

everything-

carrying an essence,

carrying a chronicle,

cold and soft,

it can never be seen

because its beauty

is a secret

that can only be explored

through the deep

sensation of feeling,

through the wise

honesty of a kiss.

Niti Majethia

The wind is always touching you,
holding you,
feeling you-
like a way of the Universe sending
out its love,
like a path the Universe takes
to express its boundlessness.

108

Nature is Complete

Nature is complete
because it invites each
colour onto its palette.
These colours are emotions-
and it accepts and decorates
each of them onto its soul.
It grows different kinds of trees,
to have a diverse forest
and then proves to us
that warmth
and solitude
can exist in the differences,
in the variety,
adding onto the richness.
Maybe the rainbow
is complete
mainly because it has
so much of each aspect of the universe,
drawing in each different colour-
filling in the different
spaces of our heart
that are haunted by emptiness.
Maybe that's what life is all about-
in order to be complete,
we need to let each

different aspect of life
paint us in different ways-
we need to come to terms with it.
We will all be so colourful.

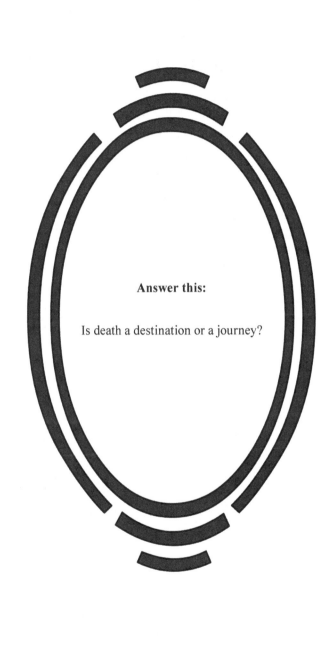

Answer this:

Is death a destination or a journey?

Real Magic

The magic is not in the way
the clouds move
to let the sun shine through.
The magic is in the way
the clouds dominate
the sun's existence
but the light reaches
where it has to,
anyway.

Remembering

The stars
are footprints of God-
and that's why they
can so gracefully
lead you Home.
The moon is a door
to a place
that teaches us
that the light doesn't need
to be everywhere-
the darkness can be beaten
just by the size
of your soul.

Shankar Bhagwan and Parvati Mata's Diary

The world is probably
a secret diary
in which God pours
his magical powers
and Emotions-
maybe we are just a poem
in God's literary journey
and we too,
hold our own special meanings,
themes and diverse
perspectives through
which we could be explored-
we are made up of meaning
and we choose our own,
rightful dictionary.

The Human Race

Our hearts connect us,
but our souls bind us
all together,
for we are all
matter of the same existence,
we are all members
of the same team,
we are all warriors
of the same country.
Our hearts connect us,
but our souls bind us.
We are all significant
creations of the human race.
We cannot be against each other,
because we are each other.

The One

But for the flower
to come in form
all the petals
have to come together.
How will our world
grow towards the grace of the sky,
towards the light of the sun-
like the flowers,
if all our petals are
never willing to be one?

The Strokes of Paint

The river is a continuous poem
written by its current,
The world is a continuous form of Art
and we are all the colours-
even while God is the painter,
it all depends on how we mix,
how effortlessly we flow,
how drops of us remain still
at some points,
what shades we create
when we fall into each other.

The Truth about Humanity

You can either

be the plot

or the theme.

You can either

be the night

or the day.

You can either

be the colour

or the fragrance.

No matter what you are,

do not judge this world.

For what you perceive

this world to be

is limited

to what your senses

let you perceive.

Have you ever thought about it?

Our only pathway

to knowing this universe

is through our senses!

There must be a million

colours that we have not seen-

another form of light,

another dimension of living!

How can we not know?

Just because we can't see it
doesn't mean it isn't there.
The world is a secret
in its purest form,
and we, the human race,
are a tiny revelation of God's heart.

Togetherness

The world
is made up of matter
and matter
is made up of atoms
stuck together,
bonding with each other.
This is the chemistry of living.
The more the human race
wishes to embrace and create,
the more we will
have to accept
and bond with each other.

Unspeakable

Then water,

what material is it?

What substance

is the sky made of?

Why does fire burn?

Is it because we aren't allowed

to touch Light?

Why does a star

appear to be so small

but still carry so many messages,

so much memory?

If the sky

is an ocean..

where is its shore?

If the sun

is here to illuminate,

why do people die of the heat?

Is death just

the climax of our story?

Do you choose your ending,

or does the ending choose you?

Is life a choice,

or do choices

together, make a life?

Knowing God

Whenever I felt nearer to Him,
those are the moments
when I would find
graceful dancing in stillness.
Those are the moments
I would find promise in truth,
a voice within meaning.
Shankar Bhagwan or Parvati Mata,
or any other God
that had come together
with all His or Her colours,
were all I ever wanted to paint with.
Those were the moments
I wanted to keep close,
when you feel nearer to Something
that the midnight skies know about.
That the ocean rings for,
that the whole system
of this universe
vibrates in forms of Love.
Every minute form of creation
would feel closer to me,
I realised this life was
to build a creationship
with The Lord,

Everything we touch and feel
is a proof that He exists,
everything we believe in
is a proof of how beautiful we are,
having place in our hearts
for not just belief,
but Faith,
the inevitable pattern
we are a part of,
a beautifully splashed together Universe.

Life calls out to you every now and then

Maybe the lightning
is a crack in the soul of the sky-
but the fact that it passes,
the fact that the sky is still together,
the fact that it has not shattered-
is a little sign from the universe
that even when there are cracks in our heart,
we can still be strong and not let it break us.
The fact that the thunder stops thundering
should tell us that our pain, too,
will one day stop paining.
No matter how hard it is to believe-
you get over it.
The colours change,
like in the endlessness
and vastness of the glory sky-
it is this endlessness
that is reflected in our soul,
in our whole system of living.

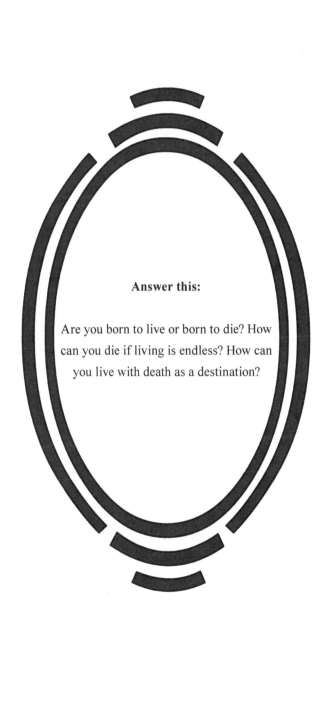

Answer this:

Are you born to live or born to die? How can you die if living is endless? How can you live with death as a destination?

The Dictionary of Existence

Maybe it isn't all that complicated.
We are all human beings,
and maybe what's most important
is that we are all here,
sharing the same planet together.
We are all going to die someday.
All of us,
there's no denying that.
We may have different aspirations
and personalities
and bodies-
but we make up one soul.
We make up the beating heart
that lives inside the earth,
and that's the reason
we are all alive.
We need togetherness
to find ourselves individually.
Not sticking together.
But being there for each other
when it's needed.
We need to understand each other
in order to understand
our own senses,
our own decisions,

our own place.
This is one heart we live in.
The beats of all life on Earth
come from the same heart.
We all have the same home-
no matter what direction we go.
We all have the same map
even though we find different
meanings in the routes
which eventually lead
us to our individual destinies.
Even though our paths may be different,
we are all using that one map,
and if we just help each other a little bit,
maybe we can all
understand the geography of life
and find our road to heaven.

The Lake of Life

A lake reflects
not in order to mirror
the surroundings,
but reflection is
in order to show
how much of your surroundings
you decorate
with your ripples
and lines,
and bring out
the image
with your own thought,
your own muse,
a bit with your own style,
for that is the purpose of life.

The Landscape of God

God is nature in its truest form.
All these trees are God.
This landscape,
this skin.
This beautiful coordination of life
while being so different,
so much coexisting variety-
breathing all together,
bringing a whole new form
of radiance
and togetherness-
if the states of matter
can exist so well together,
the water and the sand,
the liquid and the solid-
why can't we?
We are the same state of matter:
stories with wandering eternities.

The Love story of the Moon and the Earth

The moon and the earth
have the most beautiful relationship.
The ocean is their language-
science says they are both
attracted to each other.
I say the moon writes poems
upon the ocean's movements and spirit,
in order to communicate with the earth,
in order to tell us all we are supposed to hear.
The energies bring to us
a whole new meaning
of being adrift,
of being whimsical,
of being free,
within your own skin of flow.
These are the energies
that bring to us the meaning
of being in love with a soul,
so distant,
yet this language
knows no distance,
yet this time
knows no end.
And if there is no end,

what is the purpose of Time?
Time isn't to count the
stages of existence,
but to stage existence to a point
where it cannot be counted.

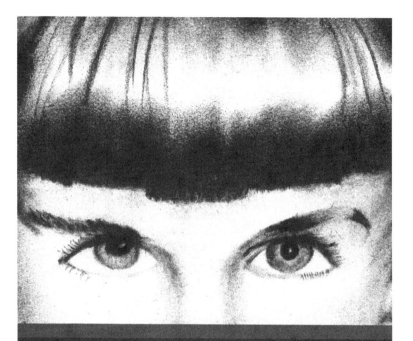

Prisoner

of

emotions

Prison of Emotions

I'm one person who has gone through most of her life yet feeling misunderstood, feeling judged and feeling like a misfit. I have a beautiful family and friends, but only I know the storms that rage within me. There are times I find it hard to breathe, the anxiety is suffocating, and it is constant- it is everywhere, every breath is pained and heavy, every single moment of life a punishment, negativity all around- I feel like there are toxins flowing out of my heart for no reason at all and all I want to do is escape it.

There are times I don't understand what's going on inside me at all; those emotions you cannot name, those are the worst. Sometimes I am broken down by the stupidest things and sometimes my heart manages to carry the heaviest weight.

People make fun of my emotions and tell me that I'm "over-reacting" or label me as weak. The truth is, nobody is emotionally weak because everybody experiences different emotions with different intensities. From what I've learnt, you cannot escape them, you cannot dodge them- because no matter where you run, you'll always end up running into who you really are, even if you try to hide it.

Reasoning sadness and depression works for most people, but quite often the mess and chaos in my head is to such a great extent that I cannot even begin to unravel the stories each emotion tries to tell me. But I've come to learn that whenever somebody tells you that you shouldn't be feeling the way you do, you shouldn't ever accept and believe that. We are all human beings and we are all striving to become the best individuals we can possibly be. Jealousy, hate, regret, negativity, these are things that should definitely be avoided for a healthy life but you are never wrong to experience them, simply because you are human. Experiencing hate and jealousy does not make you a bad person, but letting those emotions control you and force you to take wrong actions and make wrong decisions does.

I remember there was one night, right before my IGCSE board exam, I wasn't getting sleep because I was extremely disturbed by a lot of things happening around me. I felt judged constantly based on my report card, my worth was attached only to what I looked like and how I gave my exams and the tense competition of living in today's generation was building up. I felt like the people I cared about the most found it easy to ignore me and not reply to my messages. I found that people I could do anything for, wouldn't even care to think of me. I felt like I had lost. I had a paper to write the next day and I felt like I was not prepared. Worst of all, I felt like I was not enough for the world. Even today, sharing these emotions with you takes great courage because I know at some point, somebody who dislikes me or envies me may end up reading this book and will judge me all over again. But then again, I have developed this courage after I learnt what it was to be discouraged; after I realised how important courage was. This is the reality of emotions.

That night, a poem began forming within me, before I could even write it down. This happens rarely because usually the poem is naturally born as I write the first word, the next suitable word comes out without me having to think. This was a poem in me that was begging to be written, and so started writing it down in my diary.

It is within this poem that I realised and explored how many emotions I had felt in my life. My anxiety is still a problem and it kills me, it suffocates me, it is constantly looming and it's like a weight on my chest- it is something I have to deal with. With the negatives we must also remember the positives, and whether it's happiness, excitement or love- each positive emotion should be experienced in a more beautiful way, by making that positive emotion an action.

When it comes to negative emotions, get deeply into it and it becomes a prison. The hardest of all is a prison that shows you a beautiful view outside and it kills you even further because you know you cannot escape the prison and get away.

No matter what, my love,

you are allowed to be angry

you are allowed to be upset

you are allowed to be depressed

you are allowed to be a prisoner

you are allowed to feel like you're not good enough

you are allowed to feel anything and everything

simply because YOU ARE HUMAN.

Know you that you have me by your side and you will get yourself out of the mess. One day, I promise you, you will understand how beautiful you are.

So this is my opportunity, this section has a lot of darkness but deep inside of you, read closely, you may be able to find the light by relating to it.

I hope you remember that you're never alone, every emotion you feel, I am experiencing it with you, right inside, just feel my poetry and let it touch your heart and I promise I will never leave that beautiful space, I will be in every beat that it takes, to fight the negativity.

Some of my favourite lines from the poem I wrote that mystifying night include,

"Your emotions are valid

simply because you feel them.

And the most important of all:

You are human,

sweetie,

and sometimes

all you have to do is allow yourself to be."

So let's all be humans, be fragile, be anxious if our heart is in that condition, be whatever our heart demands us to be- but at the same time, once we accept these emotions, we get the strength to fight them.

We're in this fight, together. You and me.

Anxiety

The heaviness
of your heart
also shows the strength
you have
in order to carry
that weight.

Bullet

Your pain is a bullet
and you are the gun,
this world isn't a war-
there's a war within you,
and you are the weapon too.

I am a Storm

The storm
is a mix of angst
and passion-
a stir of mixing colours
and determined winds,
an outpouring of emotion
within the depth
of illumination,
forests are torn down
so that the seeds disperse,
there is lightning
cast to show the world
what it's like
when the line of a poem
is written straight from the heart,
it is striking,
powerful
and the thunder
is all the movement
of the mind.
And this,
this is the storm of life.
How does nobody see this?
How does nobody realise
that a storm

is a way of life

expressing its own inner stirring,

its own inner life?

How does nobody see

that a storm is a form of expression,

the lightning,

the change of colour,

the winds-

and we must allow life

to express itself as freely

as it wants to,

because at the end of the day,

this, in itself, is a revelation

of the real beauty within our very existence.

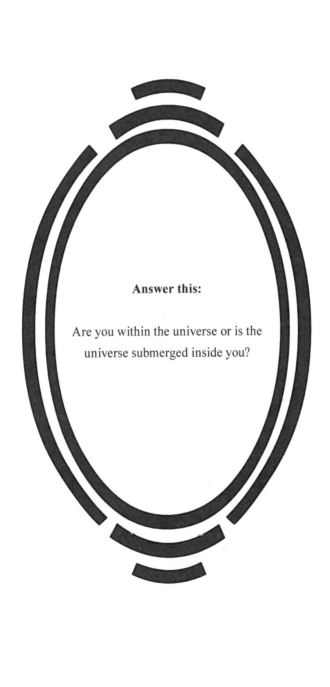

Answer this:

Are you within the universe or is the
universe submerged inside you?

Loneliness

I am so lonely,

and I am so lonely in so many ways.

It isn't even normal.

But then again, what is normal?

Is it the standardised

average based on statistics?

Are there any statistics

based on loneliness?

Are they even true?

Do people speak the truth about their loneliness?

Why do people lie?

Where are the people?

The humans?

The real ones?

Is there anyone at all?

……………………..

This is how lonely I am.

I have been left over and over

and I'm tired of missing.

I try to search for answers

without any map

but every broken bridge

reminds me of you.

Every rain storm leads me to your name,

but you still live in my heart,
you still live here.
Maybe that's why I'm lonely,
because I'm already full inside,
yet so empty.

The Cracks of Love

If you are the star,
I will be the light.
I want to be teeming inside you,
I want to taste you whole
and cover you in my own essence.
I want our minds to touch,
I want an interface of longings
to grow in the garden of our hearts.
I want to blow a fire in your ribcage
so that every time you breathe
you remember my warmth.
I want to leave the most
precious part of my heart
back with you.
And this is what it is to be in love,
to be vulnerable,
to be cracked.
But if these cracks
are made by you,
I take them to be lines
of a poem you have written for me,
a poem that holds a rhythm
and music just in its own fresh voice.

The Universe's Diary Entry

Maybe the half moon
is another page
of the universe's diary
and it holds so much pain
that describes its craters,
it holds so much loneliness
that describes its isolation,
however-
all this holds so much
substance and learning,
all this pain
holds so much value-
that this pain
has now been converted to art,
and has become an invincible
lantern of strength
for the deep voyage
of darkness.

Personal journals

And I thought I felt death.
Grubby handed,
sharp and determined-
it wasn't burning,
but it hurt-
like a whole knife
had torn my soul apart.
I felt numb
and helpless,
everything around
me shattered.
I felt like
a dumb-struck woman
falling deep
inside a vacuum
of absolutely nowhere,
and nobody cared.
Who would care about
a suicidal destruction?
I swear,
I knew I would die that day.
I felt it.
It was the end.
It wasn't about
the cause of the pain-

it was the unbearableness of it.
I couldn't keep going through this,
it didn't seem possible-
but somehow my body sustained,
and I kept breathing.
I don't know how.
But my heart kept beating.
Death mocked me
again and again,
but my body kept going.
I don't know how-
I didn't stop breathing,
and I think at some point,
my own body saved my life.

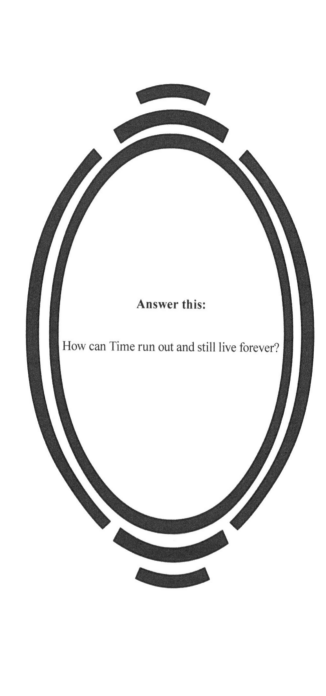

Answer this:

How can Time run out and still live forever?

This is only for You

I don't even know how to describe it,
the unspeakable and inexhaustible
feeling of being attached
to someone's soul,
to someone's whole existence.
It is painful and beautiful.
It is like tying yourself to a cloud
and you feel the rain all over you-
kissing you all around,
but at the same time,
the cloud drifts away
and quite often
you can't move with it.
Where do you keep
those who mean a lot to you,
even though they are
just a memory of the past?
If people can stay
alive in memories,
you will be here forever
I will keep you safe
in my invincible
body of light,
the body hidden
deep inside my soul,

the soft secret
that whispers your name.
The memories and past we've had
will forever be a spark,
so sharp and luminous,
holding more weight than
an entire bonfire.
I hope when you read these words
you will understand
that they were meant entirely for you.
I hope you will remember,
I hope you will reminiscence
all the old and rich tales of life
we have lived
and held amongst us
like journeys in dark shadows.
Even if we never have
any connection in the future,
there is an incomprehensible
connection amongst the stars
that still glow with the light
of our good hearts
and the spectacular flame we were,
both of us together.
There is still a flame
that not just lightens
but spreads warmth,
inside me.

I will hold onto our memories
and let them reveal
their magical music
amongst the light
of our lives
and our friendships together.
Even when we drift apart,
I hope you remember
that we still live
under the same sky
and if you look hard enough,
if you look deep enough,
if you remember me
with all your heart,
if you just look
deeper than what it is,
all those colours
will seem to you of meaning-
all those lights
in the sun
will bring back to you
the truth about believing,
you will find me in the swirling wind,
you will find me like a song
your heart-beat sings.
You will remember my words of essence,
on your wedding day,
because I told you someday

you'll be happy in love,
someday, someday.
Most of all, remember me
not for the sound of the wind
but for the way it hides itself
yet makes its strength and touch felt.

Mind games: The strange life

I play mind games with myself. Games that I should not be playing. I try not to. I hide, I lie, I create scandals in my own life, involving nobody but me. I am my own scandal. I destroy myself, pick the pieces back up and hope the light will pass through, because haven't you seen how light passes through shattered glass and makes it look like a hundred teeming stars? So I just escape. I find ways to tear apart the cage of this mind, the prison of this body, the undermining weight of this being. My impeccable taste for this life. I am a poet. Did this taste come to me or did I evolve from it? Because I am a natural phenomenon in this form. What a strange and beautiful life it must be. Oh! Except that it also isn't. It is a horror. All of this. Everything. My mind. My head. My heart. Yet, everyday we wake up and a miraculous flow of energy passes through each of us and there are conscious, vibrant vibes that go through our translucent souls as we smile. Is this not life? Oh, and yet what a disaster it is. All of it.

Who is a poet? No, ask me WHAT is a poet. If you ask me where I'm going, just like Rumi said, I am going where I came from. I am finding my soul before it was in this body. I am searching for the blood before it met my veins. I am searching for the wind that grew the first tree and held pollen in its cold but warm arms for the first time. But there's a price to pay. A price that has already killed me. But I am trying to find meaning in this dark death. In the broken alterations of my breathing. I am

155

trying, I am trying, I am mystifying- I am dying, and sometimes this death makes me take birth again.

I am trying so hard to live. I wonder how somebody else would react if they realised they were such strange creatures. I am looking out, looking in, looking everywhere- I am trying to make something of my mind that speaks of dark things based on meaningless theories. I am afraid. I am afraid to talk of this. I am afraid to talk about my mind. I am scared of myself, don't you see? So I won't. I won't say. But I will talk of the heart-beat that lost its sound. I will talk of the rains that could kiss no ocean. I will speak of the ruthlessness that hurt everyone. I will speak of the blood that will never meet a vein. I will speak of truths that can change all of the game. Do you hear me? Do you even understand? Are you a stranger, or are you a human? Or are you like me, a convergence of the two? A convergence of the infinite species of revolting life? Of rage? Of fright? Of restlessness, of exploring the boundlessness of the night?

Promise of Eternity

A Promise of Eternity

The day I turned seventeen, I decided I wanted to do something very different. I didn't want to bring in the eighteenth year of my life in the usual way. I had been wanting to do something like this since a very long time: randomly place little chits of paper with beautiful quotes by me, for some stranger to see and feel better about their day. My friend gave me this idea, of using sticky notes instead. I fell in love with this idea. I realised that I didn't want to write my name on the notes; even though my second book was coming out, I didn't want this to be about publicity. I wanted to make somebody feel happy, or at least feel something, even if it was just for a moment. Because even when you can't be a big part of everybody's life, you can make somebody feel big at least for a minute part of their life. So I randomly placed sticky notes with encouragements in a mall, which my best friend and I visited on my birthday.

And I realised, people may or may not read those notes, may or may not be happy with them, may or may not like them. But that was all okay, as long as I had tried to make a difference to somebody's life and as long as I had tried to make somebody happy, even if it was just for a moment. Because isn't that what eternity is?

Moments that are priceless hold the true value of eternity. Such are the moments, of giving happiness, of feeling happiness, of giving love, of feeling loved- such are the moments. The moments that are the currency of living, and this currency is priceless.

I've learnt that you can feel eternity within your very own breathing, within the drifting tide of your own soul when you truly feel like you are living. And quite often, you are given all the moments, all the time in the world, but eternity is never really found. I believe eternity isn't a time period, it's a feeling. It's a feeling knowing that you've left back something beautiful, and that you have tried to make a difference. All these poems show eternity through different perspectives, through different angles- whether it's something as simple as bubbles or something as delicately beautiful as the soul's movement.

Even though we are all mortal and are all going to die someday, we all hold an eternity within is. All of us may not be able to be Hollywood film stars or discover scientific phenomenon. We may not be the most sought after celebrities. Our pictures may not be reposted on the internet by generations to come. All our names cannot be in history textbooks. But this is only the superficial way of being remembered. What about inside? What about the lives you've touched, the souls you've comforted just by being alive, the happiness that has flowed into this universe whenever you smiled? What about that? What about the hearts you've stolen, the love and acceptance you have given and taken freely? All of this will remain. All of this is what we leave back. The more, the merrier. So don't worry about being famous. I'm not saying don't try, of course, work your hardest and pursue your dream. Try to be the famous one not so you can brag about it, but so you can inspire people to pursue their dreams.

But at the end of the day, you don't need a grand funeral with presidents of the world travelling to bid you goodbye. If you have that, I am happy for you- but if you don't, remember all that you have already; all that comes with life itself.

Your life on earth has enriched the air a little bit, added more nutrition to the soil and added more emotion to the water. This is possible only when you live your life as honestly as possible, when you make the best of everything you get. So throw yourself out there and let the waves kiss your feet, let the rainbow spill from your hand and let the colours gently evaporate into the whirlpool of this universe- you are an essential colour, my love. You can be all you want to be, fierce, feisty, frisky, wild, intimate or sexual or anything you want, without intentionally hurting the world. You can be anything you like and you will always be a significant symbol of being. You are a true icon. And who can compare to a luminous figure that has added its own beauty into the richly coloured universe? Who can compare to an honestly lived life, a fulfilled heart and a grateful soul, a hungry, intimate and revealing mind, now returning home?

Death will be everything you have not yet seen- life will be everything your soul has seen before, and this is what automatically gives us our strength. We are all old beings. We are all old tunes in the long lost melody of life, of the universe. We don't always have to have the loudest voice, sometimes all we need to do is hum from the heart and add our own little magical touch, let our sound not just be loudly heard, but be clearly felt.

And this, my dear, is real eternity. This.

The feeling you are getting right now.

Bubbles

A bubble has no colour
and it eventually has to burst,
but yet people would
pay to buy and blow
their own bubbles.
Often it isn't about eternity,
it isn't about something
that will stay with you forever-
it's about the forever
you can capture
just within that one moment,
the colour that you don't see,
but experience,
within that one fine stroke of art.

Continue the Journey

The body rots,

but the soul continues its journey,

life time after life time,

music after music,

all your tunes are in sync.

World after world,

revolution after evolution,

deep inside, you hold a history

that has come from the voice of Time,

look within,

look inside-

the body rots,

but the soul continues its journey.

You are within yourself

the inexplicable

and unspeakable

pronunciation of eternity.

Dare to Disperse

It is the seed

that dares

to disperse,

to travel,

in the fleeting hands

of the unknown,

the wind,

the animals,

it is the seed

that dares

to disperse,

that gets to taste

the flavour

of a new habitat,

a new, lost, deep world,

of dreamy kisses and

new nutrients,

a different soil,

new roots.

It is the seed

that truly dares

to disperse,

to travel,

to move free,

to adapt,

to create

its own variation,

being unafraid of difference,

being open minded,

it is a seed

that dares

to disperse

that creates a luminous

change of evolution.

Answer this:

How can Love be both, about surrendering yourself and building yourself from it?

Death

Death
is just life
through another dimension,
another spectrum.
Death
is just life
through the eyes
of a different universe

Fragrant Life

Some flowers
look like they've been crumpled.
But yet, they hold colour.
They hold essence.
They hold a fragrance
that tells of timeless
enchantment,
of creation,
of a journey through
wandering, long lost,
old tales.
Yet, some flowers look
like they've been crumpled.
Maybe the fragrance
is the lesson
that the crumpling taught the flower.
Maybe the fragrance
is the moral,
the colour is the essence,
that tells us that no matter
how much you get crumpled,
you will still remain beautiful.

Inner Beauty

The power of death is inexplicable.
It just takes you away,
just like that-
and all that is left
is this physical body.
I believe that's why
when you fall in love,
you must fall in love
with someone's soul
instead of their physical body.
Because when you fall in love
with that soul,
you are falling in love
with the amount of unquantifiable life
that the person holds-
and when you fall in love
with that soul,
even though death
may take it away-
the beauty of it with you
will always stay,
even when its body rots,
the beauty will thrive.

The Truth about Eternity

Eternity is just a moment
in the history of time.
Real endlessness
is unspeakable-
listen to the beating
of your heart.
It is this same beating
that is in the constant
up and down of the tides,
in the drifting
of the melodious ocean.
The way your soul
transfers its energies
into these boundless
sources on our planet
shows how much
we belong here,
how much we have inside our soul
and what an effect that creates
upon the universe.

When I fade away

Even if I do fade away
from the vastness
of this humungous night sky,
I hope I will be
the most honestly shining star
bright in the nightscape,
bringing the soil of the moon
alive with my light,
sparking the nightingale
into believing
in the magic
that comes from its voice.
And even if I fade away,
I wish for so much pain-
an artist's angst,
that I can shoot
with all the zeal of power that I have
and during that journey,
have someone wish upon me,
have someone believe in me.

Where do Words belong?

Where do words belong, really?
Where do they come from?
Every day they are
let out in the air.
Once they are said,
where do they go after that?
Are they looking for a destination?
Are they searching for a memory lost in time?
Are they looking for a place to hide?
What gives them their meaning?
Do they define themselves
by their actions
or has God bestowed upon them
a truth about their existence?
Do they die once they have been said
and take birth when they are said again?
How do they live so well on paper?
Do they prefer living in the air
or on paper?
Do they breathe?
What do they give out when they exhale?
More than that,
what do they take in when they inhale?
What is there to inhale from me?
What is there to inhale from this world?

All there is to me
is their existence,
their secretive,
mysterious elixir
that will live on
to become a remedy
in the soul of my life.
All there is to me
is their warmth,
for I am a wordful woman,
I need no bonfire-
For I am another form of fire
blazing their light.
Where did words get this light?
Where did light find its words?
Where did the world find its home?
Where is home if not within our words?
Words lead their own lives,
and leave behind
pieces of their heart
in every poem
and story
they ever truly belonged to.

*Time and
Opportunity*

Time and Opportunity

I remember ever since I was a little girl, ever since I began understanding, reading and writing language, I started keeping a diary. In this diary I would write all that I did during the day and my reactions to various things. Then as life began to become rather fast-paced, I stopped keeping the diary. However, I went through some old diary entries today- and I realised how much I have not only grown, but also evolved. Within me, the light of my life has shined so bright and even as a kid, I was fascinated by it. But today, this phase of growth, of being seventeen, of maturity, of being stuck between "almost adult" and "not quite adult" has really showed me how much this light has illuminated my life. As I have walked the one way path of time, tirelessly without aching- I still am walking, I crawl sometimes and run sometimes, but I have kept moving and life has rewarded me with new scenic beauty at each mile.

Those diaries showed me how each little incident, each day of my life, has added a little to my whole being. Maybe I cannot consciously point out specific characteristics, but life has been a beautiful and graceful transformation and each memory, good or bad, has been a stepping stone to the person I am still developing into.

Time has a beautiful way of pushing us forward and we leave behind pieces of us at every place and every mile and we take with us stories that fill the cracks of our soul. Thus, when we look back, going deeper inside Time and in ourselves, we can relive each moment beautifully.

Each moment in Time presents us with a new opportunity, with a new horizon that shines and teems like a line of a poem. It is up to us to interpret the meaning of this line in order to seize the opportunity.

Time has presented me with little opportunities and today I realised that the little opportunities have been as important as the big ones because it is the little ones that have led me towards the big things in life.

Time lays out steps for us and different paths and I think irrespective of which path we choose, there is something within each step that is leading us to the next line of our poem.

And then what? What happens next?

The line of that poem is just a clue, and deep inside we realise that the rest of the poem is us, simply ourselves. This is how milestones are achieved. This is how we reach our destiny.

This is why it's important to believe in yourself; how else will you understand the poem you are? How else will you believe it?

I'm not trying to form an impression of me being this flawless human being who has had the perfect time and opportunities and continuously believed in myself. No. I've had very bad times - the internal struggle has been so tough - but then again, all these times have left their respect and have bowed down to me whenever I have won the battle. This is all Time working its magic upon me.

There are so many answers that we don't have, so many questions that we have not yet asked. This part of the book mainly comprises of my musings on the depths of Time; how much I have felt and released, how much I have let parts of myself grow and parts of myself remain raw.

Time to me is all about opportunity because each Time of your life holds an opportunity, and the same way, each opportunity holds a specific Time.

Life is too short to wait-
seize the opportunity by the throat
and swim within the depths of Time,
see the unblinking,
mirrored visions of Life
through my eyes.

How old are you?

Maybe our life's length
is only as long as we judge it to be,
as we perceive it to be.
Some people
find glory in each moment
and even ten years is long enough,
while some try finding
exquisiteness only in the leap years.
Those are the people
that run out of time.
Remember that moment after moment,
time is revealing itself to you.
Time is opening out its arms
and calling you Home.
Moment after moment,
all these moments are for you-
tick after tock,
as you're gracefully growing,
Time is growing older too.

Life

If we journey back into time
will we come to the point
where our soul was formed,
when our body was developed
and these little veins were cultivated
to have constant flow,
constant motion and movement
within our body,
telling us that even though
our heart may stop and sink
this body will fight till the end
to survive?
If we travel back into time,
will we then understand
what the core of our existence
is made of?
If we journey into our past lives,
will we then find
a true, heart-beating purpose?
If Biology finds
what lays inside the skin
can we find what emotion lays even
within and under this inside?
If we travel in circles
and go back every

revolution of the earth,

will we know the meaning and power

of invention, life and evolution?

How have we come to be

what we have truly become?

How will we be able to

refract the rays

of our next lives

and this life

if we don't bend forward?

If we travel back

will it tell us what angle to bend?

How do we reflect

if we haven't met the object

that is to be reflected?

If these answers all lay

dormant in the subconscious soul,

why are we trapped

in the dimension

of human consciousness?

Light of the Stars

Maybe the light of the stars
is a language
waiting to be translated-
a lost universe
amongst the depth of communication,
waiting to be revealed,
like a secretive expression,
waiting to be understood.
And because we cannot fathom it
it illuminates everything around us-
breaking through the dark,
it sheds light
upon the verses of nature
so that we at least realise
that all those are languages too,
just like the language of the stars
and the light,
and that we realise
why we balance so well
with everything,
because we are
all anecdotes of expression,
landscapes of communication,
our whole system
holds so many secrets

and love
and emotions
that make us up-
all these atoms
have come together
to form a meaning
in the dictionary
of this universe.
What kind of sentence
do we form
with this meaning?
What kind of words
are our synonyms?
What kind of punctuations
do we allow?
Are we simply here
as mere syllables?
Are any of our letters
silent?
Maybe the light of our own stars
is a language
waiting to be translated-
rephrasing it,
the light of our own stars
is a language
waiting to be understood.

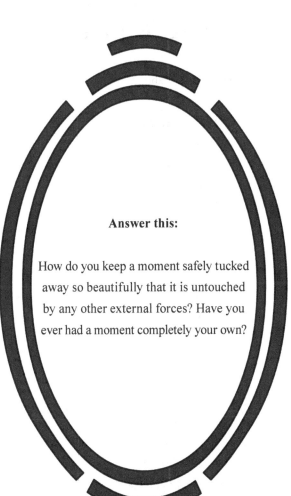

Answer this:

How do you keep a moment safely tucked away so beautifully that it is untouched by any other external forces? Have you ever had a moment completely your own?

Live your Life

Maybe life is about finding pleasure
in the small moments,
in the unexpected
surprises and the smiles,
because even a dried
petal doesn't know
when it can start
to drizzle.
Even dropped pollen
on the ground doesn't know
when an insect can come
and take it to faraway lands.
And remember
every time there is a storm
there is also a crack of lightning.
Remember
every time there is a storm
there is also some thunder.
This is the thunder
that will build up the sky-
to race ahead
in the fibrous
depth of Time.

Pathways

I wonder

why people

take change so wrongly

when we call

it growth,

so positively.

Every change

is a form of growth.

Every loss

is one step forward in

evolution.

Every closed door

gives you

the opportunity

to find a hidden key,

every hidden key

should make you realise

that some day

we too,

will all unlock

a pathway within ourselves-

a pathway beyond

the History of Time.

Rising Youth

The world
is another clockwork
mechanism
of creation-
it isn't about how well
we keep up with it,
but the depth of living
comes only from
how well we understand it.
It isn't about complicated theories
and inexplicable meanings,
it's about unspeakable silences
that have come
from the deepest root of thought,
the unspoken loves
that remain secret
for the most selfless reasons.
It isn't about the routine
and the formulae,
it's about how
well you can break the rules
and still have a solution,
because you don't find it-
you make it.
Because you don't search,
you discover.

Secrets within the actions of nature

When the flowers wilt,
they're looking down
at the soil
for a new flower
to bloom,
for a new possibility
to open up.

Memoirs

Time and memory
are so intertwined,
for memory
is a preservation
of Time,
teaching us how
to make Time stand still
but ironically
also teaching us
how fast it truly
marches away.

Nature's Lessons of Life

Each star
is an anecdote
of time.
Each little sparkle
and shine
is the moment-
each moment
we are living now
is getting recorded
in the whispering,
dense and deep
dynasty of this universe-
let your moments flow
from your heart,
live so honestly.
Let your outer worlds meet
the worlds inside.
It isn't as hard as it sounds,
you just have to enjoy
the person that you are yet to become,
feel it emerging from within.

Self expression

The world, too,
in itself,
is a form of creativity,
imagination,
freedom,
and God's self expression.
How can we then not
allow democracy
within this creation itself?
How can we not be free?

The motion of Life

Day after day
all we can hope for
is that we forget
our old broken bonds
and move forward
towards new ones.
Because even the sky
changes from colour to colour,
even the wind changes its direction-
but that doesn't mean
that it still isn't cool breeze.
Day after day
all we can hope for
is to leave back our past-
and not walk towards the future,
but walk towards a transformation.

The night sky of Discovery

The stars are buds
and the dreams
we make of them
are flowers,
the faith we
have in those
dreams is the fragrance.
The moon is a book
and the moral it holds
is within the stillness,
even though it cannot
be everywhere in the sky
it is in a place
where it is truly
blooming with
utmost passion,
and thus its light
can reach anywhere.

The real meaning of Existence

The rotations

and revolutions

tell me that the earth

is trying to move on too,

but towards what?

What is this planet

trying to develop?

We are a species

of pure creation,

of awakened spirit,

what are we here for?

Are we here to

transform the planet

or for the planet to transform us?

The human race,

the most intellectual,

the most passionate,

the most capable,

where are we letting

our intellect take us?

Are we supposed to be

taking it somewhere?

The inexhaustible,

the irrevocable,

the unstoppable.

Is our soul

the center of our being,

the sharpest of our weapons?

What is this earth

progressing towards?

Today there are men reaching the moon

and people studying the stars,

there are flags on the moon

and there are worlds

in our own different

types of castes.

We have a whole planet

in our hands,

a whole dynamic

legendary

piece of creation

directly crafted by God.

It is us God has trusted,

it is us to whom God has given the freedom.

What we make of it

is what we can add

to the whole creation

of this inexhaustible

expression of the Galaxy.

How Poems are born

Poems are born
when we realise
that emotions
are transfused in
every little moment,
in the colour of the sky,
in the honesty of a kiss,
in the way the rain falls down
and crashes into the ocean
because it can
get to dance with the tides.
For there is
emotion in the way
the sun makes even the plain clouds
feel beautiful
by shining its light,
emotion in the way
the pollen grains
leave their place
in order to explore
and hopefully
discover a home,
a place in this world.
This world is an emotion,
this universe is

a revelation of our true inner souls,

of our own inner voices

that we don't recognise.

The universe is a beating

heart of emotion

and every beat

is another opportunity

for us to make music,

to create a symphony,

to truly wake the sleeping,

to truly put to sleep the tired.

All of this is inside us.

Inside our little bodies,

lays something

that cannot be measured,

a call,

a word,

a thought,

a substance,

of substance…

The History of Time

Have you ever really felt your heartbeat?
Truly, fully, felt it?
It makes you forget about everything else,
doesn't it?
All the deadlines, the pending work-
it all melts out,
the lights dim
and you are drifting-
all of a sudden
nothing else matters.
And that is the reality of life.
This is the reality of life.
This is the thin line
where fantasy and reality meet,
this is what you were destined to be.
Have you ever truly felt your heartbeat?
It takes just a second
to connect to the galaxies-
just put your hand there,
in that rhythm is
the momentum of infinity,
like holding the truth of life.
So gracefully putting together
in a sentence,

in a beat,
in a word-
the unspeakable
history of Time.

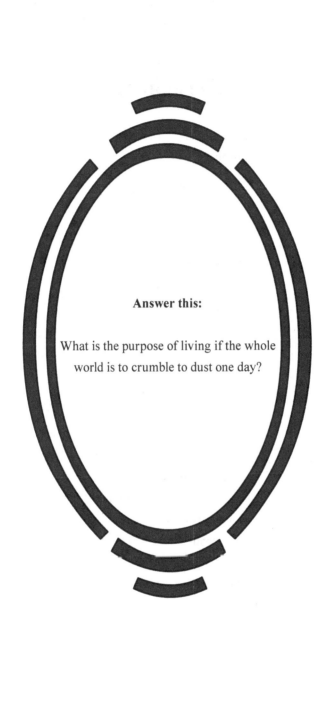

Answer this:

What is the purpose of living if the whole world is to crumble to dust one day?

The Journey

Your heart has journeyed
through Time
and within that journey
there was something
so meaningful,
so moving,
so much action-
that it slowly evolved
as a muscle and sprung to life.
You have travelled
with waves
and rivers
and softened hard rocks.
You have carried weights
in your soul
that could have crushed your body.
You have felt the whole universe
just in the palette of your paint,
and now you are here,
ready to paint.
So paint, paint, paint
as wildly as you can,
paint your dreams
and sculpt your scars,
explore your inner moon
but discover your stars.

The Recycling Bin

Because even trash
can be recycled,
it proves
that something beautiful
can always be made
from something
once labelled
as worthless.

Touch the World

The map
is the Earth's revelation,
we are the Universe's secrets-
the only way we reach out
is through our Art,
through our constant connection
with everything,
beyond what we see
in our real lives.

The

beauty of

you

The Beauty of You

In today's world, it is so easy to be judged and misinterpreted. It is so easy to feel like you're simply not good enough for anybody at all. Today, we have labels for what's "pretty", what's "hot" and what's "sexy." Today, we have labels for what's in and what's not, we label everything: people who study are labelled as something pathetic and people who don't are labelled as something equally bad. All of us look at someone else at some point and say, "She has it so much easier."

And she may have it easier within some aspect of her life, but that doesn't make everything else smooth sailing too.

MY BATTLEFIELD DAYS

I remember a phase of my life, a very personal one- but I'd like to share it with you. I had entered my teens and even though I have been writing since I was a little girl, those were the times I had actually started taking writing very seriously and began thinking about making it my career. My work had just started getting printed in my weekly school newsletter, but it hadn't been published in a magazine outside school yet. For school projects or assembly, I would write a poem and receive great praise from all my teachers. But guess what? I was targeted by my peers.

A lot of it was because I did what I did and because of who I was. I was barraged with comments like "shitty poems", "waste of space", "good for nothing" and "ugly". I had people walking up to me and telling me to stop writing; I was cyber bullied and constantly targeted.

Life was difficult. I was brainwashed very frequently to STOP WRITING and alienated for being the person I am. I won't pretend that it didn't hurt me; I'm human and it most definitely did. I became anxious and tense and it became hard for me to freely talk to people, it was hard for me to smile, it was hard for me to do anything at all. I was awkward, shy, lonely and it impacted my personality in a way nothing else had. Being brainwashed for being who I am and being tormented for writing poetry, constantly, the judgemental eyes whispering some nonsense...it became hard to even breathe. I always had my family's support so I am blessed in that way, but it wasn't easy because they didn't come to school with me. It must have been so hard to raise me, and that is why I respect my parents so much.

I became absent-minded, was never excited about anything and always loathed going to school. I had every reason to give up on writing. I was not in association with any publication. I did not have many contacts. I was just a child. But I was madly desperate. I wanted my voice to be heard. I thought that nobody in the world would ever understand how I felt. I started having outbursts. I would cry all day. I would scream. Even writing this story today instantly makes my chest heavy. I had completely lost my mind, mainly because I had no idea how to survive. I couldn't deal with it. Everyday felt like going into war. Life was a battlefield, in the literal sense. I was told that I was mildly depressed. I had just entered my teens and those were highly vulnerable years. Sometimes I thought about suicide, I thought about anything...to escape from what I was facing.

But I never did give up. Because I knew my life wouldn't endure without writing. Because only writing welcomed me. Only writing accepted me. Ironically, though these attacks were intended to push me away from writing, they actually worked like a miracle for my writing.

In order to get more solace, I'd read inspirational quotations and feel better. I started relating to them and collecting them for various reasons. Slowly I got deeply involved in philosophy because I understood a wider range of emotions: hurt, broken heartedness, low self esteem, loneliness, anxiety, depression, fear and inferiority. Melancholy understood me. Art accepted me. Art welcomed me, comforted me, listened to my cries.

My writing evolved, grew for the better because I portrayed those emotions straight from the heart. My poetry started getting more mature, philosophical and personal and since then, I have easily come to terms with making my personal life public because I believe that's what a poet does.

At exactly the right time, my parents changed my school- my new school was a lot different, a lot better. Even after the sudden shift, I took a while to heal. I still lived in fear for a while; I had panic attacks. But slowly, very slowly, it got better. I met a few people who have really contributed to the person I am today- fearless, bold and confident, with the "go-getter" attitude. These people may or may not be a part of my life in the years to come, but I take a part of them everywhere I go.

As the wounds began to heal, slowly, softly... Time went by and I got deeply involved in my writing career alongside my studies. Before I knew it, I was called to New York for my first international award for poetry, as one of the three people chosen worldwide, and my career took off really quickly and well since then.

Today, at seventeen, I have won three back to back international awards for my writing, this is my second book and I work as an environmental activist because of my poetry. I am also a public speaker and receive invitations to read my poetry at events and festivals worldwide; I will be featured in an HBO movie soon, thanks to my poetry. I also work as an editor for Kidspirit magazine and lead my very own established editorial board with a few wondrous young writers here in India. Just two years after my battlefield phase, I was featured on "Amazing kids" magazine as an "Amazing award winning writer" along with my biography, my journey and my interview.

Today, with a sigh of relief, I can say, "I made it." Maybe I'm not the most famous author yet, but I got out of the deep hole that pain had sucked me into.

I have overcome those fears and self doubting. Yes, I still feel out of place sometimes, I still get anxious, a lot, I still panic, I still get depressed but I have definitely grown and evolved. This didn't happen because of my success, my success happened because of this.

Of course there are still a lot of challenges I face and I know there's a lot more to come, but deep inside I believe in my beauty, talent and strength, thus each challenge becomes easier to tackle.

Recently, when I participated in the Uplift festival, I learned that one of my readers had specially travelled to Byron Bay in

Australia to meet me and thank me for writing and that my poetry had really given her comfort during some pained moments of her life. I also learned that there are so many people out there who have been inspired greatly by my work. More than anything, I am thankful to them for giving me a chance, because I know what it's like to not have a chance. Thus, I value it so much more.

You, my reader, no matter what generation you come from, will understand and be able to relate to the fact that all of us, at least at some point, feel like we aren't ready to get out of bed and face the world once again. The irony is that ALL of us, at some point, feel alone, and that statement in itself proves that we are not. Think about it.

There must be so many people out there feeling something similar – so what do you do on those mornings? Get back to bed? You can do that sometimes, but not always. Remember you may not be responsible for the life you have but you are responsible for the way you lead that life. For those mornings, for those moments- I have some affirmations for you. This idea is inspired by Miranda Kerr's book, "Treasure yourself" which has a lot of affirmations. Personally, her book has really helped me on dull days. Yet, being a true poet, and influenced greatly by my life experiences and feelings, I decided to write my own affirmations and share them with you in this section of the book. Read them and roll them around in your head every time a negative thought springs up; every time you feel low, unconfident or broken. I, myself, too, naturally do not always automatically follow each affirmation because I too, feel anxious, depressed, upset and uncertain a lot of times. The point is to fight those feelings with this positive weapon. When I am surrounded by negativity I use these thoughts and they really comfort me. I know if I continue to do so, they will slowly become a part of my personality and the same will go for you.

Remember, the beauty is you. It's simple. When you learn to look inside and really see how much you have gone through, how much you have done in your life- a light begins to shine. It sparkles and dazzles when you are fond of yourself and aren't afraid to show it. The beauty of you giggles from inside when you do things you truly want to and pursue your passion; your beauty blushes when you compliment it and wear it confidently- the blushing beauty thus comes out as something even more appealing. The beauty of you smiles when you accept your wounds and move on gracefully. The beauty of you especially nods its head when you stop caring about what other people think and start truly being who you are meant to be. All the powers of the world reside within you. Your spirit is handcrafted by Lord Shiva and Parvati Mata.

The beauty is you. You are the beauty. Go deep into it, and you will find a voice waiting to be heard, a voice waiting to be spoken to.

∼

Say it to yourself: The beauty of me is not in my face, my body or even my personality. The beauty of me is in the way I lead my life, the wisdom I share, the garden of my heart that grows and grows along with everything else that I have to offer to the world.

Breath of Fresh Air

How long has the wind been around?
And yet, we call it "fresh" air.
Maybe being fresh
has nothing to do with your age,
with the way you look,
because we can't see the wind,
and yet we call it fresh.
Maybe everything has to do
with how we feel
and how we tingle people
in the most beautiful way
and what we make them feel.
To me, that is being fresh,
being fresh in your mind,
your heart,
deep down in your soul.
Being fresh with life
and being fresh within life.

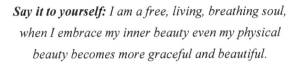

Say it to yourself: *I am a free, living, breathing soul,*
when I embrace my inner beauty even my physical
beauty becomes more graceful and beautiful.

A letter to my Readers

You are not

here to take form.

You are here to make

your own form,

to be your own

discovery of existence.

You aren't here

to answer the questions

of the stars-

but to become a question.

You are not here

to tell the world

what you mean to do,

but do to the world

something of meaning.

You are here to

become yourself,

to keep a hidden diary

of secrets

that can never be read aloud,

but are soft whispers

that are felt.

You are not here

to promise or

to please,

but to release,
to realise that
no matter what you do,
no matter what you say,
no matter what you become,
you will always be you.

Say it to yourself: *I don't let anybody control me because I am my own home and my own comfortable, constant space.*

Courage

The world
is made up of patterns.
You are a pattern yourself,
and if you will not be different,
how will your real shapes be known?
How will you diversify the painting,
how will you add a twist
to the well bound plot?
You are a pattern
embedded in the rawest
form of nature.
You are the story
the universe is secretly telling-
let your moral be known,
let your themes and motives be heard.

❦

Say it to yourself: *I don't let opinions affect me,*
because I know God loves me unconditionally and
He is more powerful than any human being.

Destiny

A lot of it is destiny, really.
Where the wind takes your seeds
is where you will grow.
But always remember
that being an essential
part of the human race,
there is no weather condition
that should stop you
from blooming.
The lotus blooms
in the dirty water,
the rose blooms
with its thorns.
The sunflower loves light
but has to bear the heat.
It is your fragrance
that will change the world-
it is always your ideas that
will intoxicate.
It is your richness
that will be far superior
to your colour
and your wealth.

Say it to yourself: *The past no longer*
bothers me because it has passed.

Flowers are You

When a flower opens up,
all its pretty petals
are vulnerable enough
to be torn apart.
But if it doesn't open up,
how will it bloom?
If it doesn't open up,
how will it sing
its song of its fragrance?
How will it blossom
if it is not brave enough
to take the rain?
How will it grow
if it doesn't move upwards
despite the heat?
How will its colours
show if it doesn't open up?
How will it enlighten
the world with its presence?
The flower makes the sun
feel talented,
the flower is the reason
the wind feels gifted,
by transporting pollen.
You are the reason

the world
is shining around you-
you are the light
because you dare
to let your
uniqueness shine.

∾

Say it to yourself: *I have no regrets. Every path I take, even if it tears the sole of my shoe, is eventually leading me towards the soul of my destiny.*

Inside

Deep inside
you will always find
magic secrets of yourself.
You may not realise it now,
but inside you is a song,
and it is your heartbeat that is the music.
It is your existence
that is the melody.
It is your very form
that is the lyrics.
You are music
in the orchestra of the world-
and when there is noise all around,
you don't have to make your voice louder,
you just have to listen
to your own quiet,
deeply.
It is in this quiet that
you will discover and become
a symphony.

～

Say it to yourself: *I am healthy because I feed my
mind and body with love, positivity and nutrition.*

Listen

Are you the quiet
in the stillness,
or the stillness in the quiet?
Do you create your own space,
or become it?
Does the world let you
inherit your own soul,
or do you let your soul
inherit the world?

≈

Say it to yourself: *I speak confidently and
smile whole-heartedly, filling the room with
the beautiful essence of my presence.*

Oranges, anybody?

The oranges
are squeezed hard
and look what happens,
they become a delicious juice
with clarity and substance,
with nourishment,
a different state of matter
with the same freshness.
So don't be afraid
when life squeezes you hard,
the state of matter
within existence
will change for the better.
There will be freshness
and clarity
but most of all,
it will also release
your seeds
and set them free.

Say it to yourself: *I take care of myself. I do what I love and wear whatever makes me feel beautiful, pretty and confident.*

You are your own Sunrise

Sometimes
when you
accidentally wake
up early
and there's nobody up
for you,
you have to get solace
from the sunrise.
Life is a lot like that,
too.

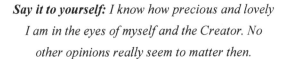

Say it to yourself: *I know how precious and lovely
I am in the eyes of myself and the Creator. No
other opinions really seem to matter then.*

Wounds are Beautiful

In order to be a scrumptious dish
that tears the world apart,
that oozes into the taste buds
and creates a magical flame,
you need to be cooked.
In order to be cooked,
you need to be able to
take the fire,
hold the heat.
Accept the pain,
the burn,
the feeling of being
born complete.
This is you
discovering yourself.
The wounds are marks
leading you to your next stop.
These are all clues
that are scattered
in order for you
to make something
of your existence.

Say it to yourself: *I trust God and the*
purpose of my own existence.

Mentality

Like the sky's colours,
you need to realise
that no matter what,
you can never control
anybody's mind,
mouth or heart.
Just remember
every colour
is an opinion
and whether you like it or not,
it's always going to be there.

Say it to yourself: *I use criticism to build myself stronger.*

Peaches

We are all peaches,
with the seed
in the center of us,
in the core of our existence-
our heart, our soul,
that is what emerges,
that is what can truly grow.

Say it to yourself: *I'm not afraid to stand up for*
myself when somebody hurts or harms me.

Atoms of being Human

The nucleus of an atom
holds positively charged particles.
Similarly, everything
we are made up of
holds love at its center,
holds positivity at its core.
We need to realise
that we will never
reach where we want to
if we don't first appreciate
where we actually are.
We are born with this heart,
with this soul-
the biggest asset of all,
we are born with
the ability to feel.
We can experience lilies
through our sentiments
if we want, we can feel life
in ways we have not yet imagined.
Open your positive heart of protons
and realise that you are not made up of energy,
but the energy is born for you.

Say it to yourself: *I am secure in my own skin. I know I
don't have to bring anybody down to lift myself up.*

Do not be lazy

But the bird cannot fly
if it feels lazy to flap its wings.
The stones cannot spark
until they rub themselves.
The moon can hide itself
but the earth keeps spinning,
there's a revolution
in our soul
right from the beginning.
Do we recognise the energy
burning inside our soul?
Or do we sit back
and weep in the darkness?
If there is the darkness
are we brave enough
to form the stars?
If there are the stars
are we brave enough to write
the poems of the constellations?
Are we brave enough to seek
the light that the stars have,
the light that becomes their ink?
And if this is their ink,
what is the poem?
Is it our soul

upon which the ink
touches and illuminates?
Are we mad enough
to see these things?
Or are we afraid?
Or are we lazy?
Are we brave?
Are we here to be?
Or are we here to become?

Say it to yourself: *I talk to people who listen to and
understand me. I always keep them very close.*

Inner Biology

The veins in your body
come out to be pathways-
your unmapped,
raw and beautiful soul.
You are not here to
give those pathways names
but to leave those pathways
with such beautiful memories,
to let your adrenaline pump so well
and fight your fears so bravely
that your name
is automatically kept after
the strength and
exquisite experiences
within those pathways.

～

Say it to yourself: *Everyday, I have my healthy "me"*
time that makes me feel happy about being alive.

Secrets of the Universe

The veins
are pathways for blood.
Look how the universe
has made pathways
for all the little things
that need to travel,
spread their nutrients,
the things that are needed
somewhere-
the plasma of your soul,
your cells of your passion,
all these little things,
are exactly the way
they're meant to be-
the universe
has secret pathways
for everything,
the world
has secret keyholes
to where you
need to be.
You just need to realise
that you are your own key.

Say it to yourself: *I apologise when I can and let go of all guilt, because I want to create a better future.*

Something to read every morning

The mystery
isn't about what the world is-
it's about who you are
in the world.
It's about how you feel
out of place
because feeling out of place
isn't bad.
It only drives you further
into yourself
to awaken a place where you belong.
Your home can only be
inside of you.
Everything else is a stop-
you are the destination.
You are born
within yourself,
but by the time you die,
you would have explored
all the little clues
and details,
understood the map
and the roads-
understood the
different clockwork system

of Time that lives
like a secret inside your body.
Don't stress over it.
That is the purpose of life.
The purpose of life is not
to get the best grades
or the most difficult degree,
or to be the richest man on the block.
Understand that
you are in yourself
your own little galaxy,
with your own rules,
your own limitations
but also your own
boundlessness.
Accept that
while sometimes things
may get out of control,
when you cannot even
handle yourself-
times like these
are times when you will
open up a new pathway.
Walk that way.
The treasure
isn't what we are looking for.
We are looking for
how well we can

understand the true
essence of treasure,
and break all the barriers
that define the word "wealth".

~

Say it to yourself: *Anything that comes my way is an*
opportunity to experience life from a different dimension.

Stillness

There is stillness
even in the quiet
beating of your heart,
there is stillness
in every matter
of your existence.
This stillness is
what helps you to understand,
it is this stillness
that helps you
with the movement of life.

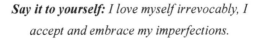

Say it to yourself: *I love myself irrevocably, I
accept and embrace my imperfections.*

The Garden of the Planet

The whole body is soil-
the stories are the seeds,
the cultivated
and most rich part
of our soil
is our heart.
From these stories
spring blooms,
flowers,
fragrance-
these are what we release
into the world,
hoping they
will find their way
with the wind-
carrying our essence,
our morals,
our wisdom,
our music.
We are in ourselves
a garden
and despite the fact
that we may all
have different flowers
and different buds growing,

we are all beautiful.
Because a lot of flowers
have thorns
but every flower
has the potential
to leave back some pollen.

∼

Say it to yourself: *Everyday, I ask God for forgiveness for anything that I have ever done wrong, and then I thank Him for all that I have ever gotten and all that I have ever done right.*

Niti Majethia

The Glories of Life

Life is so fleeting-
yet it stretches on.
Life holds so much inside,
yet, at the surface
it begins with just living
and taking each moment
as it comes.
We are all painting
our own horizon-
and whether we like it or not,
our heart is the colour,
and our soul is the shine.

~

Say it to yourself: *I wear what I want to wear
without worrying about what others will think,
because style is a form of self expression*

To be a Woman

Ladies,

wear your flaws

like your trademarks,

with so much grace

and wholeness

that they become

a style statement.

Let your essence

become your walk.

Let the light

of your soul

become your talk.

Let your wounds

remind you of the magic

in raw nature.

Let your soul's tears

remind you of rain

that grows crops.

∾

Say it to yourself: *When I express myself creatively and freely,*
I do justice to all the gifts and wisdom God has given me.

Warrior

Camels have long
eyelashes to protect
from the sand
going in.
Creatures are coloured
a specific way
to provide camouflage
from predators.
God sends us all out
into this world
as warriors,
completely equipped
not just for survival
but also to seek
the nutrition of life.
And the truth of the matter is
that even if you cannot find it,
you can always create it.
Don't underestimate yourself.
The strength in you is as heavy
as the weight of existence,
and the weight of existence
is phenomenal-
the whole world
depends upon it.

Remember you hold
so much within you,
so carry yourself gently-
for you are a seed,
everything around you is here
to help you grow.
It isn't about how much light there is,
it's about how much you absorb.
It isn't about the house you can build,
but the home you can create.
It isn't about drafting maps on the earth,
but embracing the guidance of the stars...

Say it to yourself: *I let go of things that are not in my control and trust God knowing He will do only what's best for me.*

Welcome Home

Everybody can build houses-
but it is your soul
that can build a one of a kind home.
The home that welcomes you
no matter what,
a home that reflects
the light of the universe
and a home that is written
like a constellation
from the shine of the stars.
This home is eternal.
It can only be made within you,
like a dime
that has given
you so much richness,
like a river that has
given you a path
to overcome all the rocks.

Say it to yourself: *The iconic value of my existence lies only in my own hands.*

Hunger

We all need to find that tide-
something that will bring us
to our answers at the shore.
We all have it within,
it smiles secretively
as the ocean within us
begins to roar.

Say it to yourself: *God believes in me. Why else would He have put me in this universe, if I didn't have the strength to fight?*

Short stories

In the night of life, if all the birds turn away into their own little nests and refuse to sing, let God be your nightingale, let the moon be your song, let the starlight be your melody.

(( ))

The law of Chemistry and molecular substances teaches us that in order to be complete, we have to form bonds, we have to donate and we have to learn to share.

(( ))

Maybe the real question is whether our life is a question that comes to us as suspense or our life is an answer waiting to be truthfully revealed.

(( ))

The only Time is the clockwork of your heart, the only true smile is the meaning of your soul.

(( ))

Art is the earth's biggest secret wonder, a lingering question to which human existence is itself the answer.

⟨⟨◉ ◉⟩⟩

Anxiety is the heart knowing answers- but not understanding the questions.

⟨⟨◉ ◉⟩⟩

Adventure is your heart taking off on a vacation within the dormant, vast and boundless horizon of human existence.

⟨⟨◉ ◉⟩⟩

Like the sand and the water, our hearts are all made up of different states of matter- but look what happens when the sand and the sea meet, there is something so soft that comes to form.

⟨⟨◉ ◉⟩⟩

We are the stars and God is the moon. Even when we stop shining, our sky will never be without light.

⟨⟨◉ ◉⟩⟩

You left me with unanswered questions and unspeakable answers.

《◎ ◎》

We are here to journey deep inside the moist and bruised skin of the universe.

《◎ ◎》

Life on Earth is an example of how being weird and completely different from all the planets can spark something beautiful.

《◎ ◎》

Life is all about questions- it isn't just about answering them, it is about discovering more than a solution, it is about making your own kind of formula.

《◎ ◎》

You are your very own signature, your passion shows how much you understand this sign.

《◎ ◎》

Evolution comes through struggle so we remember how important it is.

(( ))

The clouds are ideas and the rain is the poem filled with inspiration, and look what honest writing can do- it can help a plant bloom, it can help the garden of the soul blossom.

(( ))

Our map is a crumb in this universe. We will travel to where we belong if only we start to realize where we are.

(( ))

Maybe our lives have our own kind of maps and the real challenge is uncovering the territory you never imagined could even exist.

(( ))

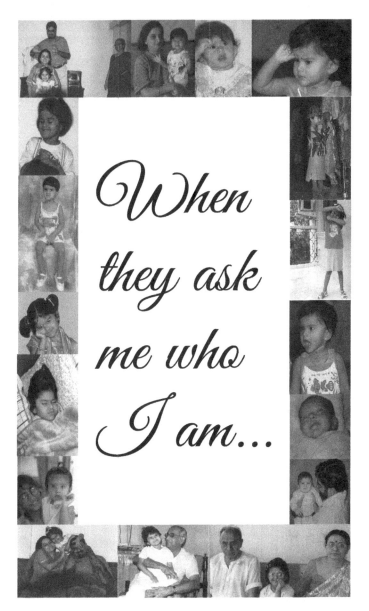

When
they ask
me who
I am...

When they ask me who I am

She was living in her own daydream, all the time, every time- of deep conversations with soft and understanding people and the hungry rain, of expressive storms and poetry and whole kisses and the completeness of living, of wearing the glamour that her own brand chose to wear. For she was in herself a brand, a brand of her own- her own kind of living was all she could live, and she did not stop for anyone or anything. She laughed unapologetically and loved unspeakably, gave her all to what she loved- she felt loveable even when she was always unloved and infinite even when she was in the prison of society and its rigid expectations.

She wasn't the A* student when it came to every subject nor was she the perfect girl that every single guy wanted because she was a butterfly and the real colours of her pretty wings showed only when she truly decided to fly.

In order to meet the ocean she had to flow boundlessly as a river, and she knew she could soften the rocks with her wetness.

Home was just echoes and languages and distant, dreamy smells of the system she truly lived in. Lonely and alone and lost always in her own magic secrets, she was never the rock you saw on the dry shore, or even the wet shore- she was the rock you found deep inside the core of the earth in the ocean, with crystal and colours that were never seen before. It's so hard to explain this to people sometimes. So when people ask her who she is, she only says her name... hoping someday it will be able to do justice to who she really is underneath.

When she loved, her blood held every strand of every lost ocean, craving the shore, the stir of passion was not a mere longing, but a song that wanted to be heard but couldn't find the music, couldn't find a voice, to sing the lyrics.

So she stood up and sang even though it didn't sound right at first, but now it has become a melody that can be heard, even in the sound of the lightning.

So the next time, don't ask her who she is, but what she is.

Even in the complete loneliness she will find love in the shadows, if she must.

Even in the blood and wounds she will find beauty because she understands how much of the universe is immersed in her whole body to make up all that skin and flesh.

This is not just something science can explain- even in her long lost stars she will find the light and make a constellation, if she must.

Even when she fails she will win because she will learn from why she failed.

So the next time don't ask her who she is, ask her what she is.

The beauty isn't because her lashes are dense and defining or her hair is long and lustrous; the beauty comes from the fact that she can wish upon her lashes and she can believe in herself.

The dark mists are just adding to the strength of the mountain and the different colours of life add to her sunset.

For they add to her palette and now she can paint so much more- today isn't even about the striving, it's about the growing within the striving.

So don't ask her about her strife- ask her about the growth.

All the tears she has spilled have caused a river on its way to meet the ocean of life, every day is a new rock she softens, and even if she doesn't soften it, she moves forward with her current.

Most of all, she holds a secret world inside all the flesh and muscles where the beating is a drifting tide pushing her forward; these magic secrets are a formation of all the sparks that have not burst into flames, but died down.

To those sparks that never had the chance. She collects them with her stardust fingers and let's them free- like voices and echoes that call the universe in its mother tongue.

She dreams of landscapes with so much freedom and fulfilling kisses with the real magnetism of being alive and boundless.

She breaths for the times her heart discovers its own inner wilderness, when her love for spring finds inside her rib-cage a new species of blooming flowers, despite the fact that her soil is not fertile enough, despite the fact that she feels unloved sometimes.

And even though sometimes her wounds become like tunnels within her life, even though she has a rough past, even though she couldn't carry the weight of her heart at some point in her life, even though love made her weak, she believes there is strength inside the weakness. Sometimes when you can't find the strength you have to become it. Her roots will forever be entangled in the hearts she first actually felt beating, even though she has gracefully stood up and moved on. Her life is an assortment of all sorts of pasts, presents and futures- her life is a collection and she is simple yet inexplicably complicated.

She is sharp and resonating, confident and unapologetically passionate. She doesn't know if she believes in loving a man or any external human being, for that matter; she is an inner terrifying and mystifying world that needs to be understood in order to love.

She is not an experience. She is a discovery.

She's drifting but also journeying.

She has no beginning and no end.

Unspeakable.

Invincible.

Inevitable.

Niti Majethia

About the author

Seventeen year old Niti Majethia is a back to back international award winning poet from Mumbai, India. She started writing poems when she was just a little girl and over the years, her love for literature has grown and so has the depth and beauty of her work. Her innate ability to perceive and express emotions and thoughts fearlessly, along with finding beauty in the ordinary, supported by her twisted, strange and intimate relationship with the universe, is what makes her work stand out from the rest.

Extremely accomplished, despite her youth, she has won three international awards from Kidspirit magazine, for which she later established an Indian satellite editorial board and worked as an editor. Besides winning other prizes, another notable point in her career until now includes being featured by Amazing Kids! Magazine as the "Amazing kid of the month" for August 2013.

Her poetry has taken her to wondrous places around the world and presented her with opportunities to touch the lives of many. As an Earth Guardian, she is also a public speaker, with her poetry to be featured in an HBO movie soon. She was invited last year to read her poetry and talk about the environment at a conference held at the United Nations headquarters in New York. She is one of the five youth leaders chosen from all over the world to launch the Global Alliance of Youth in Action portal (GAYA), to which she donated the proceeds of her first book "Imaginiti", which was auctioned at the UPLIFT Festival at Byron Bay, Australia.

She is currently pursuing the International Baccaleaurate programme at RBK International Academy in Mumbai, India.

CONNECT with Niti: To get more of her poetry, quotes, other forms of writing, updates about her career (including the availability of her next books) and appearances she may schedule near you, please Like her official Facebook author page: www.facebook.com/NitiMajethia. You could also see glimpses of her work on INSTAGRAM: www.instagram.com/ nitimajethia.

Index of Content